Dear Freddi:

Letters from Angels

Dear Freddi:

Letters from Angels

FREDDI T. LANE

Chasen Dreams Media

ISBN: 978-1-7366024-7-8 (Paperback)

ISBN: 978-1-7366024-5-4 (Hardback)

ISBN: 978-1-7366024-6-1 (Electronic)

Library of Congress Control Number: 2024905623

SPECIAL SALES

Freddi T. Lane's books are available at a special discount for bulk purchases.

For details visit: www.fredditlane.com

DEAR FREDDI

DEDICATION

Hebrews 13:2 NIV

"Do not forget to show hospitality to strangers, for by so doing some people have shown hospitality to angels without knowing it."

DEAR FREDDI

Table of Contents

DEAR FREDDI

SERIES INTRODUCTION

Preparing this series was a real journey towards self-discovery for me. While writing the third book in the Creating Your Lane series, I experienced a mental block that prevented me from completing the book. Something deeper within me was brewing. Stories from my past, about my identity, created a brain fog. I did not know what to do until I heard familiar voices from heaven, encouraging me not to give up and continue what I had started.

Listen, negative influences are real and can cause you to derail if you allow them to take up space in your head. So, as I've traveled down this literary path towards healing, I've had the chance to share my perspective about my pure feelings, emotions, and true thoughts in the "Dear Freddi" book series, this series is my take on embracing positivity, accepting inspirational guidance, following your intuition, and spreading empowerment.

I have experienced a rollercoaster of emotions while writing these books. But it's been an incredible journey, and I'm so grateful for the chance to share this unique form of literary therapy with you. Through these polyphonic epistolary methods, I've opened up and let you in on the transformative story behind this series.

The "Dear Freddi" series is a fictional project loosely using situations from my own experiences and journey towards healing. It shows how we all try to accept ourselves and heal. I believe many people will connect with this journey because it's about self-affirmation and not seeking validation from others, which is something we can all understand.

I've had more therapy sessions in the past few years than ever before. You name it, they've got it covered in therapy from - family therapy, marriage counseling, therapy for overeaters, therapy for debtors, you name it. I am not ashamed to admit that therapy has helped and continues to help. Through this journey, I realized nothing beats one-on-one therapy. It's because this helped me completely. I didn't need any other therapy. Because let's be real, once you figure out how to handle yourself and your thoughts and emotions, everything else just falls into place.

It would be dishonest of me, both to myself and those around me, if I ignored the fact that certain issues from my past need to be addressed and talked about. As a black African American female, many of us were raised to embody strength and independence, with a mindset that we do not require help or guidance from anyone.

It is not uncommon for people to be taught that the details of their lives should be kept private and not openly spoken about. I understand everything is not for everyone, however, what if there are things, we've overcome in life that can help others?

In our society, we are often conditioned to suppress our emotions and continue forward without acknowledging or confronting the deep wounds caused by abuse, trauma, abandonment, and the challenges that life presents to us. I realized through therapy that I constantly seek external approval to validate my existence.

Honestly, I was an emotional mess during my teenage and early adult years, and even times now, which is why I had to learn to be okay with not needing others' approval to live the way I wanted. I wanted people to be okay with me, so I changed how I acted and tried to fit in, even though I didn't want to. I was told to sit up, be still, don't cry, be quiet, act right, or else. I was always worried about what others thought of me and the choices I made. When I was younger, sometimes I would rebel and do things my way, but I always got punished.

Now, as an adult trying to work through the process of being a wife and blending two families, I find myself triggered by my past, again trying to prove myself to others. It seems worse now because I am pushing to prove myself to people that I know don't care if I'm here or not.

In my past, but even more today, I feel like I was always living in the shadow of what others expected as if my voice didn't matter. I know I'm a good person, doing all I can to support others when I can, but

I'm the only one who hears or sees me. Experiencing and hearing this pushed me to the extreme in my efforts to show people different ways of doing things and living life. It was like hearing that person's voice in your ear, always pointing out the negatives. But you're just trying to show them you're a good person, and you don't have to live life their way. A lot of this stuff comes from the generations before us and gets passed down, even if we try not to do the same things. It upsets me that as a parent; I caught myself doing and saying the same things that hurt me when I was younger and even as an adult.

Through my therapy sessions and professional relationship with my therapist Trina, my trusted therapist, I untangled important facts about my life history. This journey allowed me to re-visit my childhood, teenage years, trauma, adulthood, parenting, death, and marriage. With Trina's guidance, I embarked on a transformative journey of self-discovery—one where judgment was replaced with support, and guidance gave way to the tools needed to help me along my journey down my path.

For the first time in my life, I pivoted through therapy. It was a day that would become the foundation for the healing and self-empowerment that I would ultimately experience. Trina, being so wise, assigned me a simple action that would forever alter my path to self-acceptance. We used to talk about how you can't please everyone or get everyone to like you, and I knew that.

Trina told me to write direct and heartfelt letters to the people who I felt had caused pain in my life or influenced the negative thoughts I had for myself. I bared my soul in the letter, finally saying all the things I've kept inside for so long. The letters were pretty long and stood for my heart, yearnings, hurts, pain, and feelings. However, what happened next was unexpected and held great significance.

After pouring my heart onto the pages, Trina told me to burn the letters. I considered burning the letters quite foolish because I had put time into writing them and all I wanted to do was deliver them personally. At that specific moment, as I re-read the letters, I felt an overwhelming sense of contentment and satisfaction, as I finally expressed all the thoughts and emotions that I had been longing to say in exactly the way I wanted to express them. I made it clear and described how much I was hurting in the letters. It was important to me that the people reading them fully understood how sad and upset I was.

I followed the instructions and burned the letter, releasing my feelings. Watching as the words turned to ashes and were carried away by the wind. I know it sounds crazy, but this cleansed me. Trina said that no matter what was in the letters, the person would never understand the message. It did not matter how many letters I wrote, or how many times I cried, begged, or tried to prove myself to them as a good person because their feelings for me will be just what they think of me. This purification and explanation to me held an incredible power—the power of closure.

Through the act of writing and burning those letters, I discovered something profound. I found closure within myself, an internal acknowledgment that I had released what needed to be released. Though the words were never delivered to their intended recipient, they had served their purpose, and I was free to move forward and be relieved of the mental pressure that burdened me with wondering why.

This experience ignited a spark within me, one that would lead to the creation of this book series. In a reversal of that therapeutic technique, I wrote a series of hypothetical letters—not to others, but to myself. Adding a little fictional imagination, the hypothetical letters contained a powerful mix of closure, inspiration, encouragement, apology, and self-acceptance. These letters have taken on a significant role in my life, acting as a lifeline that provides me with strength and affirmation, ultimately guiding me toward a future that is filled with more brightness and positivity. My goal is that maybe this series will help others and maybe even encourage others to create similar stories.

DEAR FREDDI

BOOK INTRODUCTION

"Dear Freddi: Letters from Angels" is a book that offers readers an inspiring and touching experience, as it is filled with both encouragement and heartfelt messages. In this specific release of the series, I am embarking on a captivating voyage into the celestial realm, where I am blessed with the opportunity to receive heartfelt letters from family members, close friends, and beloved individuals who have passed away. This book is a collection of recipes of remembrance and hypothetical letters.

These letters provide me with the support and guidance to navigate the highs and lows of life. As I go through life, doubting myself sometimes, the wisdom and love of these guardian angels give me peace and a connection to those who have passed. This is a form of affirming the greatness in my life and the blessings that I've received.

Hopefully, the reader understands how human relationships can touch the heart, showing that even in death, our bonds with loved ones remain unbreakable. "Dear Freddi: Letters from Angels" is a devotional that shows the power of love and offers a healing method for affirming your greatness. This book has helped me, and I hope it can also help others with finding a method for dealing with acceptance.

DEAR FREDDI

CHAPTER 1: A LETTER FROM GRANDMA LIZZY

Dear Freddi,

How are you, my most spoiled grandchild? I bet you are surprised. I bet you never thought in a million years that you would receive a letter from me. I would like to acknowledge that there have been times in my life when I have faced struggles in expressing my emotions. Back in my heyday, things were completely different from how they are now.

In the 1940s, me and my sisters went to school, worked, and never moaned about the struggles of life. We walked to school in the rain, snow, and sleet, never complaining because we did not have any other options. We had to go to school or be punished by momma and daddy. We were four tough women, and I guess we passed that down to our kids.

Vivian, the wild sister of the bunch, always seemed to be caught up in trouble. In school, the catholic nuns, who were our teachers, always whacked her on the hand. If you got on her bad side, boy, she could cut you with words using her sharp tongue. You reminded me a little of her. Up here she's calmer. You know the Big Guy has a way of bringing peace to our hearts.

I grew up in a small country town in Southern Maryland in a typical black family where we lived along long dirt roads, clotheslines in every backyard, and homes where there was always something good cooking on the stove. Things moved slowly and relationships were everything. In our town, we all knew each other and were raised to live simple lives, settle down, start families, and succeed by living life with what we had. The fact that we had dependents relying on us made it imperative for us to avoid living beyond our means.

I met and married Emmit in the prime of our lives. He was tall, dark and handsome and I was fine as wine. With 13 children, our lives were undoubtedly busy, as we worked hard to provide for our growing family. Thankfully, our oldest child, your mother Tori, stepped up and played a crucial role in helping us raise her younger siblings.

Tori was daddy's girl. Emmit and I clashed whenever I wanted to correct Tori for some of the things that came out of her smart mouth, but Emmit was always there to be her protector. I used to ask Emmit; what type of child do you think she will be if you never correct her? He looked at me and said, "my child". "She will be known as Emmit's child" and no one shall ever punish her. As you can imagine, that caused disagreements between me and Emmit. Our two oldest children, Tori and Emmit Jr. were my husband's pride and joy. The funny thing is we nicked named Emmit Jr., Pride, and called Tori,

Joy. The nicknames were fitting because both were untouchable in Emmit's eyes.

You were our first grandchild born to Tori and her boyfriend. The day you came into this world, my heart was filled with so much joy and love that only being a grandparent can compare. The arrival of the first baby in our immediate family brought happiness to us. Your aunt Carol held the title of the youngest family member until you were born, with a 10-year age difference between you two.

It was great seeing you grow up, despite the bumps and bruises along the way. I remember how you scared us when you fell from the bunkbed at three. I'm sure you were jumping on the bed when you broke your leg. You were a little ball of energy. You had this huge cast on your entire left leg, but you didn't let it slow you down. You didn't let the cast on your leg stop you from moving around with your little three-year-old body. You've always been determined to keep pushing for what you want. Our struggles with bathing you while you had the cast on were quite the adventure.

The years flew by, and I had no clue we would become even closer. I'd sometimes watch you while your parents were at work. There were days when I'd invite you to my work world at the Hen's House Diner. I loved cooking at the Hen's House Diner, making meals that were good for the body and soul. Living near the local army base, we fed people from different backgrounds and cultures. Our busiest time was during lunch, feeding hundreds each week.

The moments I had with you were the highlight of my work. I'll never forget when we had dinner together, just you and me sharing a fried chicken plate in the front seat of the family wagon. Those memories mean the world to me. I can't forget when you pitched in to make biscuits for the busy lunch shift at the diner. We were standing side by side, you on a step stool, both wearing matching aprons, making those biscuits that everyone loved.

You were my amazing apprentice, ready to learn all the wisdom I had to offer. You'd hide in the corner of the kitchen while me and my buddies handle the chaos of the diner. Cooking together made our bond unbreakable and showed how much I loved you. I loved how curious and mischievous you were, just like me. You were such a curious child, always up to something, and I loved you for it.

But our time together didn't just end at the diner. We face tough times, but they make us who we are. My hope was for you to grow into a powerful, kind-hearted woman, inheriting the wisdom of our family. I spent so much time with you, teaching you all about cooking, sharing remedies for sickness, and lessons on respect.

Hey, remember when your mouth got a bit too sassy? I'm sure you remember those times when I had to lay down the law and would have you go out back to find your switch? It wasn't a punishment because we were mad, but to help you learn to respect and grow as a person. After spanking you, I gave you a tight squeeze and whispered words of love while you were crying. I wanted to make sure you know that I still love you, flaws, and all.

Remember when you called your autistic Aunt Anne a hussy, just because you heard it on TV? When I heard you say that I immediately made you go to the bathroom to wash your mouth out with that big piece of ivory soap that everyone used. Yeah, laugh, but I bet you can still taste that gross soap. You learned your lesson because you never said a bad word around me again.

Time went by in a flash and life was just happening, and you were getting taller every month. You started spending more time with your dad's family, so I saw you less. Unfortunately, there were no young girls around for you to have fun with at my home. Your dad's side was all girls, and they always had sleepovers and were close.

I remember the last time we saw each other. Your mom brought you to visit me in the hospital after my stroke. Vivian, my sister, was braiding my hair while I was lying down. I heard you coming and looked up to smile and say hi. I thought that was the first time you entered a room with Vivian, and she didn't say to me "Little pig with big ears". We had an unspoken rule not to discuss adult stuff because there were kids around. I don't remember everything, but I do remember smiling at you and seeing fear and love in your eyes.

During that hospital stay, I passed away not long after your visit. I get it didn't make sense to you when you saw me because I was not hooked up to any machines or anything. Turns out, God had other ideas. I had another stroke and ended up in a coma after you visited. I was in intensive care, hooked up to all sorts of machines and tubes. The doctors said my organs were failing, and I was basically brain dead. Your granddaddy, your mom, and all my kids had to make a tough call that day. They chose to take me off life support, but it was the right call. The doctors were right. I was brain dead and God had already taken me to spend eternity with him.

I'm up here watching you and thinking about all the memories we had together. It makes me so happy and proud to watch over you. I always wanted more time with you there on earth. I want you to know that even though I left this world when you were just a little nine-year-old girl, I've been watching over you and praying for you every single day. You've become one hell of a resilient woman. I saw all your wins, your vulnerable moments, and how beautiful you are inside. Your hair looks great because it's naturally beautiful, just like mine. Every milestone you reached made me so proud, knowing that you are continuing to create a great legacy for our family.

You've always been amazing, causing people to think differently when having those deep conversations. Your passion for business and determination to succeed touches the hearts of all who have the fortune of knowing you. When I see how far you've come, I'm amazed by the incredible woman you are. You've nailed it by not being afraid of showing your wisdom, but also by showing humility. Even though I can't be there in person, my spirit is always with you. I walk beside you, silent and feeling proud. I'll be by your side when you're feeling down, offering comfort. You'll always be my first mischievous granddaughter; our hearts are forever connected.

Just know, my love, that you're carrying my legacy. Face life's challenges head-on, knowing you've got the strength and wisdom of those who came before you. Your journey is unique, and I am honored to have played a part in shaping the incredible woman you've become.

I love you so much and I'm so proud of you,
Grandma Lizzy

DEAR FREDDI

Lizzy's Honey Butter Biscuit Recipe

If you're curious about how I make my buttery biscuits, look no further as I am about to unveil the secret recipe. When you were a little one, you used to help me make these biscuits that you loved. I hope that these biscuits are shared with your family and the recipe is passed down to generations yet to come.

Ingredients:

2 cups all-purpose flour

1 tablespoon baking powder

1/2 teaspoon baking soda

1/2 teaspoon salt

1/4 cup cold unsalted butter, cubed

1 cup cold buttermilk

Honey butter Ingredients:

1/2 cup unsalted butter, softened

1/4 cup honey

1/4 teaspoon vanilla extract

Pinch of salt

Instructions:

1. In a medium mixing bowl, add the softened butter. You can let the butter sit at room temperature for about 30 minutes to

soften. Add the honey to the softened butter. Add the vanilla extract and a pinch of salt. The vanilla extract enhances the flavor, and the salt balances the sweetness of the honey.

2. Use a fork to combine the ingredients. Mix until the butter, honey, and vanilla are well blended and smooth. Set the mixture aside.

3. Preheat your oven to 450°F (230°C). Line a baking sheet with parchment paper.

4. In a large mixing bowl, whisk together the flour, baking powder, baking soda, and salt. Add the cold cubed butter to the dry ingredients. Use a pastry cutter or your fingertips to work the butter into the flour mixture until it resembles coarse crumbs.

5. Make a well in the center of the mixture and pour in the cold buttermilk. Use a fork or spatula to gently stir the mixture until just combined. Do not over-mix; the dough should be shaggy.

6. Turn the dough out onto a lightly floured surface. Gently knead the Dough a few times until it comes together, but still looks somewhat rough.

7. Pat the Dough into a rectangle, about 1 inch thick. Fold the Dough in half, then pat it down again. Repeat this process until you begin to see flaky layers.

8. Use a floured biscuit cutter or circular drinking glass (about 2.5 inches in diameter) to cut out biscuits. Press the cutter

straight down without twisting to ensure proper rising. Gather any scraps, pat them together, and cut more biscuits.

9. Place the biscuits onto the prepared baking sheet, leaving a small amount of space between them.

10. Brush the tops of the biscuits with the honey-butter mixture. This will help them brown and develop a nice crust.

11. Bake in the preheated oven for about 10-15 minutes, or until the biscuits are golden brown on top.

12. Remove from the oven and let the biscuits cool on a wire rack for a few minutes before serving.

13. Serve your freshly baked buttermilk biscuits warm, with some honey butter

DEAR FREDDI

CHAPTER 2: A LETTER FROM GRANDDADDY EMMIT

Dear Freddi,

How are you doing, girl? I can't believe I am writing this letter to you. I saw Lizzy writing, and she told me I had to get writing because we are your lifeline here in heaven. We help you through the good and bad times that you may be going through down there. I can't put into words what I am feeling writing this letter to you. My heart is filled with so many feelings of happiness.

Even though I died unexpectedly from a stroke when you were just eleven, I always knew in my heart that Tori would hold the family together. Let's be real. She was in charge of the family from a young age. That is my fault and I apologize. Lizzy and I would clash because she tried to correct Tori and I wouldn't have it.

Tori had a way of always telling people what to do and she would respond in anger when you did not follow her rules. Our children would play school and Tori was always the principal of disciplining the children. We would come home from a night out with family, only to come to find that Tori had all of her siblings, along with her cousins, lying on the floor playing "nap time". Some of them fell asleep. I guess that was her plan. I can laugh because that was Tori for you.

Sometimes, as parents, we don't see the problems we've created until it's too late to do anything about it.

Hey, remember that the family loves and appreciates you. We didn't express our feelings with words, hugs, or holding hands to show love. But in anger and disappointment, it was a different story. We always found a way to tell a person off. We were taught this and damn, I wish we had better tools to un-teach it to our kids.

You're the oldest granddaughter, so it's on you to keep our family traditions alive and pass on our traditions. I know it's a struggle for you because of what others have said, and how you feel you've been seen because of your differences. I can tell you're just tired of some things that used to work for us, that you don't agree with them. I agree with you from up here and I see that some things we let happen, like arguing with and fighting each other, add to the bullying by our children.

The aggressiveness that is shown by our family is not always necessary, but to unteach it became hard after everyone became adults. I didn't know it then, but now I see our way of dealing with emotions and the tactics used led to physical and mental abuse, trauma, and unhealthy relationships. I see how generational tactics have a long ongoing effect, especially in your generation. I guess I should be glad that you're trying to get help, so your kids and future generations don't go through what you did. We all know they'll have a lot more to deal with. So, working to get rid of some of the negative generational stuff will help.

Looking at you makes me so proud to be your grandpa. I gotta admit, the way I see how you handle life, in my day, you would've been called a weak woman. You are full of emotions and will cry at the drop of a dime. You seek counseling, and your need to talk about your feelings and hurts is hard for some people to understand. In my day, there was no whining or pouting about what we did not like, and we taught our children the same. There was no time for any of that. We did not have time for what we saw as being weak or feeling sorry for ourselves. Life was tough enough dealing with everyday struggles.

Looking at you and how you are dealing with the relationships you share with others; I should have shown more tenderness towards my wife and children. No, you are not weak, damn, you're the strongest woman I know. It takes guts to be open about what's bothering you. You are open to the world inviting all types of comments, both positive and negative. You're doing awesome, owning your flaws, and going after what you want. It's so different from back in my day.

When I was growing up, women weren't as independent as you all are now. I see how you're motivating your daughters to do well in their education and careers. Gotta say it's not something we saw a lot of in my day. I remember when your momma, Tori, came to us with the ridiculous idea of joining the military. Without hesitation, I told her that it would not be possible. Now that I know better, I realize that our earlier beliefs came from not knowing any better and just our sense of not wanting to know anything different.

Even as a military veteran myself, I believed that only homosexual women wanted to join the military. I strongly opposed the notion of my children being labeled as homosexual in any manner. Even if I had a child that thought he or she was gay, they had better not show those feelings in my house. A man was a man, and a woman was a woman. There was no in-between. Looking back to then, that wasn't right, but now I see that time has brought about changes.

It is interesting to observe how society has evolved, allowing people to live freely. In this community, people of all sexual orientations, whether gay or straight, live together in peace and acceptance. I see what we called "transvestite" even walking around living life freely. I believe you all use the term transgender now. In my day, something like that would not have happened. I have noticed that your generation has made significant strides in allowing individuals to freely express themselves, which is good. However, there seems to be less support and care for one another. This is very different from what we experienced during my generation.

Growing up on Greenmount Avenue in the inner city of Baltimore, Maryland, I learned to appreciate the small things in life. It's worth knowing that your grandma, Lizzy, who is from the country in Southern Maryland, and I have both grown up with the same family and community values as we put in you, our children. You are special to me, Lizzy, and your aunts and uncles because you are the first granddaughter and the only one that I have the chance to spend time with. Your cousin Nash arrived two years after you and it was pretty much you and him for a long time. Your other cousins, well I have watched them from above and see so much of me and Lizzy in each one of them.

The day you were born brought us so much joy, it's impossible to put it into words. Ever since you showed up in my life, it's been nothing but happiness and love. We all waited at the house, excited, until your mom brought you home. I felt proud and hugged you tightly. Even though I couldn't walk, my upper body was okay.

During the prime of my life, I found myself confined to a wheelchair. My lower body paralyzed and left disabled from a shot from friendly fire, while at our post in Australia during World War II. Since I was home during the day and your grandmamma was working, Tori would bring you over to hang out with me. You'd be glued to my side, with the TV blasting. I'm looking back at the day when you were supposed to be on the sofa watching cartoons, but your uncle Kirk took you

34

outside and let you drive his car. I believe you were 9 years old driving that big old sedan up and down the street. I thought to myself now what will Kirk tell Tori if that child gets hurt?? Your uncles would let you do anything.

Being a disabled veteran, there were days when old veteran buddies who served in the war with me would come over and visit me at the house. You would look at them staring at the metals on their jackets. We would hang out for hours, smoking Pall Mall cigarettes and sipping Kessler's whiskey. We'd share stories about our Army days. Those afternoons meant a lot more to me than just my old army buddies dropping by to chat about the good old days. They also reminded us of all the tough times our generation's veterans went through and the special connection we share. Even though we fought for our country, when we got back home, they treated us like we did nothing, like I wasn't in that wheelchair as a result of being at war.

I remember just wanting a beer at the local bar, but they wouldn't let me in because I was black. I was so mad that I called my brothers to meet me. I saw two options: either I was gonna get that beer while sitting at the bar in my wheelchair or my 8 brothers were gonna wreck that store. Yeah, that plan wasn't the best, but once my brothers came, I got my beer.

I see y'all dealing with racism, but I hope things don't go back to how they were. I don't get it because in your time there are so many people with parents of different races, so it's hard to believe anyone would be racist. Take a look at how the slave masters helped shape the different colors in our culture. Seriously, why is racism still a thing? We're all God's people, so let's love one another.

After that incident, I kept to God, and I was always so grateful to him for allowing me to live in the first place. There were times when I felt frustrated and insecure about my ability to walk, despite the occasional setbacks, I made a conscious effort to keep an optimistic outlook. I've had a lot of moments where I've dealt with depression and sometimes ended up drinking too much. I mean, I was a man, and I was stuck in a chair, not able to work. But I always found comfort and restoration by leaning on God. I relied on God and was always thankful to him for giving me the chance to live. I found that by praying to God; I was able to keep a positive mindset. I even began to watch those preachers on TV.

The holidays were truly enjoyable for me, mainly because I had the chance to attend midnight mass at church with my family on both Christmas Eve and New Year's Eve, which were definite highlights of the season. It made me happy to see you attend your very first New Year's Eve mass last year, which is also referred to as the Watch Night Service.

The Watch Night Service I witnessed you attend at your church was much different from what we experienced at our old Catholic church. Although we did sing and move a little, what I experienced at your church was more than that - it looked like you were attending a full-blown concert, and you all loved it. If we had done something like that during my day, we would never have been able to make it back home. Who needs a club when you've got church? I danced right beside you and saw you, Roger, and Zack having a blast, dancing, singing, and having a great time. It's great that God is the center of your family. Keep prioritizing God.

I was a real inventive man, always trying to figure out a quick way to get things done. I wasn't a handyman like your dad, but I knew how to get things done. The incident that occurred at the bar resulted in my brothers and me earning a newfound level of respect throughout the county. I made some cool friends, some were black, and some were white. Dewy Elkridge was a good white man that owned a car dealership. He was friends with both me and your other grandfather, Percy.

Do you remember the day I called up Dewy Elkridge to get your Aunt Carol's first car? You couldn't believe it! After I did all the ordering on the phone, Dewey's staff would bring the car to my house, and I would sign the final paperwork from my living room. I'm looking down on you now and I see you guys doing the same thing but on your phones. That was my invention. Now you tell everybody that.

I used to wish I could be there to tap you on the shoulder and help you through tough times. I gotta say, I'm so proud of how you've decided to deal with your problems. You know, sometimes you stumble and need a little help, but I've noticed you're getting closer to the Big Guy, and it's paying off. It all starts with finding a good church home, and it looks like you've got that covered. Life is like a victory flag made of love, laughter, and lessons. And oh, what vibrant colors you have added to that flag!

I'm filled with pride seeing what an incredible person you've become, with your parents' support and God's strength. The work you are doing in public service, aiding, and supporting others, is truly outstanding. It filled me with pride to witness your dedication to serving veterans, as well as your efforts in collaborating with others to ensure that they have access to the medical devices they need to improve their daily lives.

I noticed that you displayed a strong passion for the field of prosthetics. Your involvement at the wheelchair clinic, where you selflessly aided veterans in getting comfortable with their devices, seemed to bring you a great deal of joy and satisfaction. It is truly an honor to see that you are working to provide support and raise awareness for people with disabilities. I am also honored to know that my situation as a paralyzed man may have influenced some of your actions. As I watch you and all of my family thrive in this life, I am filled with joy and dancing with happiness in the heavens.

When I see your life, I don't just see a simple woman. I see a strong and caring person who inspires others. I was so happy when I saw that you founded an organization to help people with disabilities. Thanks a lot, and the clients you'll assist will be grateful for your support.

I am here, just like now, when you need to want to laugh, cry, or cheer. I am here to support you. My spirit surrounds you, during all your ups and downs, and in-between I am here cheering you on.

Love you,
Granddaddy Emmit

Green Valley Peach Tea

Share this recipe at the next family reunion. It will surely remind everyone of me while leaving them with just the right amount of freshness needed during a hot humid day.

Ingredients:

2 oz Kessler Whiskey

4 oz brewed peach tea, cooled

2 oz peach schnapps

1 oz lemon juice

1 oz simple syrup (combine equal parts water and sugar, heat until sugar dissolves, let cool)

Peach slices, for garnish

Fresh mint leaves, for garnish

Ice

Instructions:

1.   Brew peach tea according to package instructions and let it cool to room temperature. In a shaker, combine whiskey, peach tea, peach schnapps, lemon juice, and simple syrup.

2.   Fill the shaker with ice and shake well to chill and mix the ingredients. Fill a glass with ice and strain the cocktail mixture into the glass.

3.   Garnish with slices of fresh sliced peaches and a few mint leaves for a refreshing aroma.

4.   Stir gently and enjoy the delightful combination of peach tea and whiskey in this Peach Whiskey Iced Tea.

DEAR FREDDI

CHAPTER 3: A LETTER FROM GRANDDADDY PERCY

Dear Freddi,

How are you doing gal? Just saying and writing your name makes me happy. Your parents honored us by naming you after our family, the Freddirichs. Just thinking about me and Margaret's family gets me all emotional. Our family is amazing, and it makes me so happy to know everyone is doing well.

I was told that men shouldn't cry, and if they did, they weren't considered manly. Boy oh boy, how wrong we were way back then. I know it's hard to believe, but let me explain why I'm emotional. Just a few years before I died, Margaret was in the hospital and the doctors had given up on her, saying there wasn't much they could do. My children, especially the girls, were adamant that I don't give up. They encouraged me to speak out and make sure the doctors did everything they could to keep Margaret with us for many more years.

That day I wanted to cry. I wanted to go to the corner of that hospital room, hug one of my children, and cry but I did not. It's annoying how people still believe black men are weak for crying. From that day on, I vowed to express my emotions, and I did until my last breath. Growing up and even as an older man, I had to be strong for the family

44

and that came with pressure. Your daddy David understands the pressures I'm talking about, and it can get to you.

Can you believe it's been 15 years since I died? Man, things are so different now. Can you believe it? The fools are still acting foolish and the selfish are still being selfish. You remind me a lot of your aunt Trudy. Both of you are great women, adventurous, and can be fierce when provoked.

Growing up, I was a country boy raised on my family's farm. The place right where your parents' home sits today, on Love Ranch in quiet Southern Maryland. When I married your grandmother, Margaret, her brothers helped me build our home with our bare hands. We built it brick by brick on the Chesapeake Bay in Rich, Maryland. It was there where me and Margaret's home stood, a place where family and love thrived.

Margaret and I came from large families, so it was natural for us to have a lot of children. We had 13 children naturally and adopted and fostered over 20 other children from the community. Coming from a large family, it tickled me to know that your dad, my son David, would only have one child. But to be honest, girl, you were a handful. You were like the boys, bad little rascals, but David always knew how to handle you. From the moment you entered this world, you were his pride and joy, and you could do no wrong.

As a hardworking man, I dedicated myself to supporting my family, passing down the values of working hard, saving money, being kind to others, and always looking presentable to my sons and daughters. I was known as a handyman, repairing broken furniture around the house to build our family's forever home. My work spoke volumes about my character and my determination. In a predominantly white community, my work and pride were a testament to the equality and respect I believed in, breaking barriers of race and prejudice in our community.

It gives me pride to know that my entrepreneurial skills were passed down from me to your father, aunts, uncles, and now you and your cousins. We tried our best to show your dad and all our children that nothing is given to you. You have to work to make money to support your family. The biggest thing I learned is that there is always a service that needs to be fulfilled that can be turned into a business. I was one of the first Black owners of school buses in our county. I contracted my buses out to schools in the county, which was a business that my daughters continued after my retirement.

I was a member of the Black Chamber of Commerce and other organizations in the county and state, which helped to empower entrepreneurs and people that needed support. That is why it makes me happy to see you and your effort to always empower those around you to build a business. So many people will make the excuse of their race holding them back. Some will make excuses that being a single parent hinders them from opening a business. In a time when racial tensions were high, I was able to grow as a businessman, which is why I see it as nothing short of making excuses that these young people make instead of building their dreams. You are different and I praise your parents for allowing you to grow and allowing that entrepreneur gene to grow in you.

I believed in the power of God, education, correction, and guiding my family to become the best people they could be. Keeping God first was always a staple for my family, as we praised and worshipped God. As you know, I served as an Eucharistic minister, serving the people who could not make it to church for communion. Margaret and I made every effort to attend church every weekend. When we took you and Cheryl with us to church, you would always fall asleep in the pew and Cheryl would pick up your head and put it on her lap. You and Cheryl were truly sister-cousins growing up. Volunteering for the lord was never anything our family fell short of, and I pray that you and your family continue to be active in church and community. I am proud to see you working with the food pantry and volunteering with the teens at your church. People have no idea how blessed you feel after working for the lord and god's people.

That said, I'm not going to end this letter without chuckling a little. I still laugh when I think back to the days of when you were younger. You know you were a rascally little thing. I recall that time when you overindulged on eating some white grapes. You ate so many grapes, just eating one after another, then about an hour later, after eating all those grapes, you kneeled over with belly pain and stayed in the bathroom for hours. Now at the time, we only had one bathroom in the house, and you had it tied up. I was mad because Margaret and I were trying to get ready for bed and you were held up in the bathroom. By golly, you jackass! I yelled, "Why did you eat all those grapes?" A few days later when telling David, all I could do was laugh. Just thinking about it now it brings a smile to my face now, when I look down upon you and the rest of the family to hear them mocking me and my colorful language.

It is through these seemingly unconventional moments that I hope you understand my love for my family. Every correction, every punishment, was rooted in a desire to see you all grow into respectful, responsible and compassionate individuals. My love was not always direct, but it was there. My love was shown by making sure there was food on the table, making sure the lights were on, and making sure everyone had what they needed to survive. It was a love that believed in your limitless potential and looked to guide you and my entire family toward greatness.

There were times when you, Margaret, Cheryl, and the other girls made space in our home for me to have meetings with my Knights of Columbus brothers. After we set up and the brothers arrived, I would see you out of the corner of my eye, sneaking around the corner, ducking under the tables, being nosey to hear what we were discussing. Despite your grandmother perceiving you as mischievous, I saw you as a curious and eager-to-learn girl, which is why I couldn't help but smile. I bet it was something to see, a group of black men meeting to talk about business. Making change showed some serious strength.

I often look down on you and others and wonder if my purpose in life, was to teach all my children and grandchildren. Every moment spent with you all was an opportunity to impart the wisdom that had been passed down through generations. I hoped to have shown you through my work and the work of your father the values of compassion, hard work, entrepreneurship, and respect for others.

I find relief in the fact that my teachings took root in your heart, helping make you an innovative businesswoman. Those who don't know you will know you and your heart as you carry the principles of empathy and entrepreneurship, spreading knowledge to those around you. I am filled with pride as I witness your dedication to making a positive impact in the world. Recently Margaret and I smiled as we listened to a serious conversation you and Roger had during dinner about maybe fostering a teenager. Giving hope and a home to foster children was your grandmother's passion, and it became mine as well. You are living up to the legacy we left behind and I am most grateful. Life had its challenges, but our family bond was unbreakable. Even in my passing, I check in on you all.

When you were just a young girl in elementary school, one of the hardest tasks that I had to do was to tell you that your grandmother Lizzy had passed away. I remember you waking up and coming out of the kitchen. You were never an early riser, but you got up early that morning. You went to the bathroom and washed your face and hands as you did each morning. Then you came and sat in my chair at the head of the kitchen table. I don't know but maybe you felt something because you never sat in my chair, especially on a Sunday morning while Margaret was preparing breakfast. You sat in my chair wearing an oversized white T-shirt. You tucked your feet under the t-shirt and sat there not saying a word with your head looking down at the floor. I was hanging up the phone from talking with your dad while he was at the hospital. He called to tell us that Lizy passed away and he asked me to tell you the heartbreaking news. I didn't know how to tell you because, at that time I don't think that I ever had to tell anyone that young that a close loved one had passed away. I was not an emotional man, so I rested my hand on your right shoulder and told you that everything would be okay. Then I told you Lizzy died. You were speechless, but tears began running down the sides of your cheeks. Margaret came over from the stove to give you a big hug.

Death is something that we must all go through and seeing you and our family by my bedside and again beside Margaret when we took our last breath filled my heart. Everyone was united in peace during those times of sorrow. Remember how I stayed with you all until I was able to have closure with all of my children? You all stood there in disbelief, seeing me take my last breath moments after Percy Jr.'s children visited my bedside. My work was done, and there was nothing more for me to do there on earth, but now I am rejoicing in heaven living without pain or illness.

I'm not sure when I will be writing again. So, I can't end this letter without letting you know that I happened to catch a glimpse of you attempting to recreate my sister's renowned grape wine recipe. It was quite an experience to see you in action within the confines of your apartment. I couldn't stop laughing. A few weeks later, during a Sunday dinner evening, the most amusing moment occurred when you decided to bring out the wine, and your uncle George, after taking a sip from the bottle, made a face of disgust. The wine did not taste good at all, but David was able to improve it by adding some sweetener.

Seeing all of you enjoying yourselves, laughing, and joking around brings me joy. It's hilarious to see you guys trying to copy our family recipes from root beer, wine, and stuffed ham to potato salad. It's unfortunate that we didn't write anything down and relied solely on memory. However, please don't be discouraged and continue your efforts. You already have the main ingredients and with time, you will master all those recipes. Just keep trying and don't hesitate to share your culinary skills with future generations. If there's one thing we have learned from our experiences, it is the value of documenting information by writing it down. This is a lesson that we would like to share with you and for you to share with others.

Witnessing the incredible transformation into the woman you are today is truly amazing, and I will always carry a deep sense of pride. Remember, you're never alone on this journey. I am here always to pray beside you on business ventures, and travel, and support you in every push you need to help people build more businesses. Me and Margaret, we pray and believe every day; you witnessed it. Since the day we got married, Margaret and I promised to kneel every night and pray together, thanking God for our family's blessings. I appreciate seeing you and Roger pray each night. I encourage you to continue praying and believing, as I am excited to witness the positive impact of prayer while also excited to see the good trouble you will create.

Though my earthly journey has come to an end, the love I hold for my family is eternal. I ask you to continue embracing life with the same vigor and determination that I admire in you. Chase your dreams fearlessly, knowing that you carry the essence of our family's love within you.

Love to you all,
Granddad Percy

Percy's Blackberry Wine Recipe

This is my sister's wine recipe that I would you to make. Make a batch of this wine just after Halloween and I promise by Christmas it will aged so that you can enjoy it with all of our family.

Ingredients:

10 cups fresh ripe blackberries

7 cups granulated sugar

1 packet wine yeast (suitable for fruit wines)

1 teaspoon yeast nutrient

Campden tablets (sodium metabisulfite) for sterilization

Water

Winemaking equipment (fermentation vessel, airlock, siphon, bottles, etc.)

Instructions:

1. Prepare the Blackberries: Wash the blackberries thoroughly and remove any stems, leaves, or debris.

2. Sanitize Equipment: Sterilize all your winemaking equipment, including the fermentation vessel, airlock, and any utensils you'll be using. Campden tablets can be used for this purpose.

3. Mash the Blackberries: Crush the blackberries to release their juices. You can use a sanitized potato masher or your hands.

Be gentle to avoid breaking the seeds, which can release bitterness.

4. Place the mashed blackberries in the sanitized fermentation vessel.

5. Add sugar and mix well until the sugar is dissolved.

6. Follow the instructions on the yeast packet to activate the yeast.

7. Once activated, add the yeast to the blackberry mixture. This helps ensure a healthy fermentation.

8. Cover the fermentation vessel with a sanitized lid or cloth and secure it with a rubber band. Place an airlock in the lid to allow gases to escape without letting air in.

9. Let the mixture ferment in a cool, dark place for about a week, or until fermentation slows down.

10. After the first fermentation, siphon the wine off the sediment into a clean glass container.

11. Repeat this process every few weeks until the wine is clear and no longer producing sediment.

12. Once the wine is clear and fermentation has stopped (no more bubbles in the airlock), it's ready to bottle. Use sanitized bottles and corks.

13. While you can enjoy your blackberry wine shortly after bottling, it's recommended to let it age for several months to allow the flavors to mature and mellow.

14. Store the bottles on their sides in a cool, dark place.

15. Once your blackberry wine has aged to your liking, it's time to enjoy the fruits of your labor.

16. Serve it chilled and enjoy the rich, fruity flavors of homemade blackberry wine.

DEAR FREDDI

CHAPTER 4: A LETTER FROM GRANDMA MARGARET

Dear Freddi,

How are you and my girl doing? I'm sitting here, thinking of my children and grandkids. I get so happy when I think of all the good memories. It has been only a few years since I entered heaven. Not a day goes by when I don't have thoughts or check in on y'all. Today, I wanted to set aside doing crossword puzzles to write this letter.

It is good to know you are married and happy with Roger. I remember the conversations we had about him, and I always thought he was a good guy. You two would visit me during the week, spending time with me as I watched my soap operas. I would dose off and when I would wake up, I would see Roger over on the sofa sleeping just like me. I laughed when he told me that my sunroom was so comfy and warm that he could not resist falling asleep. He said the sofa was calling him. It brings me joy to know that he is now a part of our family. It also helps that I always heard him tell you I smelled good.

Thinking back to your childhood, I would like to clear up some things. I see thinking back to Christmas' with us, you thought I loved you less than the other girls. That is because I gave gifts and presents to your other cousins and never gave you a gift at Christmas. As an adult, you know Christmas is not about gifts but as a child; we know all children look forward to gifts. When we did not give you any gifts, that led to your frequent feelings of sadness and the misconception that I did not love you. I don't know, maybe I should have given you a little something, but I did not.

Your grandaddy and I talked before getting gifts and agreed that your parents, David and Tori, went above and beyond to provide you with absolutely everything you could ever imagine. You were so lucky to have two great parents who loved and adored you, your entire childhood to even now as an adult. I had complete faith that they would take care of your material needs with no hesitation. So I gave your cousins some extra love during Christmas because they did not get whatever they wanted. You have been truly fortunate throughout your entire life. And don't forget, you were Emmit and Lizzy's only granddaughter, and they all spoiled you like crazy. I hope you can understand my intentions and know my love for you never fell short.

Beyond the presents, our bond was strengthened through the love of cooking and me trying to teach you to sew. I shared with you the secrets of my good recipes, including those crab cakes that have proven difficult to replicate since my passing. Every Friday, as a family, we sat down together to savor some delicious fried fish, a tradition that seemed to live in all catholic family kitchens on Fridays, especially during Lent. This connected us, seeing your eager eyes soaking up all of my actions, watching me scale the fish. Afterward, you and Cheryl would take the scales and place them against your nails as if they were fake nails. You saw me using the simplest ingredients to season the coating for my fish. You soak up the culinary wisdom of duplicating my recipes in your kitchen.

As a homemaker, I also had an immense love for children. I enjoyed every visit from you and the other grandchildren. When you lived with me at five to attend school, I enjoyed watching you and Cheryl. You were like a little sister to her.

You were a bad little girl, always getting into trouble and keeping me on my toes. Percy Jr. used to call me and ask, what is badness getting into today? I remember the day I got on you for jumping on the bed. I hollered, "Stop being a little devil, and stop jumping on that bed!" As I reached out to grab you while you were jumping, I accidentally scratched your eye. I laughed as you threatened to tell your daddy, my son, David. You were on a mission to get into everything, but I still loved having you around.

I remember one-day washing clothes and telling you to stay away from the washer. That is because it was a dangerous machine. It had a rolling feeder that was used to ring out the excess water from the clothes. Well, somehow you disappeared from my sight and went to play with the washer. Not noticing that you had disappeared, I heard this loud cry and screech. I rushed down to the laundry room to see your arm was stuck in the feeder. The machine was pulling you up off the floor. Thank goodness that your older cousin, Jordon, was there. He ran to the machine to hit the emergency release button to release your arm. I believe that was a learning lesson for you because you never went close to the washer after that incident. Oh, the memories that are etched in my memory of those moments of mischief!

As you grew older into adulthood, our conversations became opportunities for you to pick my brain and soak in the love I had for you and everyone around me. I recall the conversations we had about my willingness to open my home up to the foster children I cared for. Similarly, it warmed my heart to know that you embraced Roger's children as your own, extending your love and compassion to them. As a mother of 13 children myself, adopting and fostering other children, I know there are challenges with raising children. I would be telling a story if I did not say that raising, guiding, and disciplining those that were not naturally minded was easy.

Remember when you are working through the process of blending your families that you may not see the effects of the love that you are trying to pour into them until years later. I see your struggles. I remember you told me, "Grandma, them kids hate me". I told you to be patient. Also, I said his daughter was like you, she is a daddy's girl. Now your relations with Roger's son I see are different. He is truly the baby of your blended family and will have more time with you than the others. Continue to love and guide him. I do believe he sees that you are there to support him.

Now my girl Raya, you have done a great job with her and as single parents I praise you and Cheryl. You and your girls make me proud. I see you both doing what I taught you and one of the things is showing love through food. You both ensure that your families are served a hot meal every day, cooking with love. I pray you continue to love and pray over your family. These simple moments, filled with love and warmth, are the ones I hold dear.

I want you to remember the love that surrounds you. Carry the lessons I taught you, the values of prayer family, love, compassion, and kindness, in your heart. Embrace life's joys and face its challenges with strength. Roger's love for you is a testament to the remarkable woman you have become, and I know that together, you will conquer any obstacles that come your way. Percy and I kneeled and prayed every night before going to bed. Keeping God centered in your life will supply comfort.

Although I may no longer be physically present, my spirit is still by your side. Whenever you need guidance, look within your heart, and you will find me there, whispering words of encouragement and love.

Love you!

Grandma Margaret

Momma's Atlantic Fried Croaker Fish Recipe

This is my easy recipe for my fried fish which was caught fresh and enjoyed every Friday.

Ingredients:

6 whole Atlantic Croaker fish, cleaned, scaled, filleted

1 cup all-purpose flour

1 teaspoon paprika

1 teaspoon garlic powder

1 teaspoon onion powder

1/2 teaspoon cayenne pepper (adjust to taste)

2 tablespoon Old Bay Seasoning

Salt and pepper

Peanut oil, for frying

Instructions:

1. Rinse the Atlantic croaker fish under cold water and pat them dry with paper towels. Seasoning the fish inside and out with salt and pepper. Set it aside.

2. In a shallow bowl, mix together the flour, paprika, garlic powder, onion powder, cayenne pepper, and Old Bay seasoning.

3. Heat a large skillet or frying pan over medium-high heat and add enough peanut oil to cover the bottom by about 1 inch.

Dredge each fish in the flour mixture, pressing gently to adhere. Shake off any excess flour.

4. Carefully place the coated fish in the hot oil, making sure not to overcrowd the pan. Fry in batches if necessary. Fry the fish for about 3-4 minutes on each side, or until they are golden brown and crispy. The cooking time may vary depending on the size of the fish. Use a slotted spatula to carefully flip the fish halfway through cooking.

5. Once the fish are cooked, use the slotted spatula to remove them from the oil and place them on a plate lined with paper towels to drain excess oil.

6. Serve the fried fish hot, with your favorite hot sauce.

DEAR FREDDI

CHAPTER 5: A LETTER FROM AUNT TRUDY

Dear Freddi,

Hey there, my crazy niece! It's your Aunt Trudy checking in from the pearly gates! I know you're probably thinking, "Trudy, what on earth are you doing up there?" Well, let me tell you, darlin', heaven ain't half bad, and I'm up here, strutting my stuff, beautiful as ever and my spirit that's still as sassy as ever. Just like on earth, the angels up here love me, it's because I listen to them. Not with judgment, but with a friendly ear. But Jesus told me to tame it down and pray for myself and all of you down there!

I couldn't help but hear you talking about me down there, and I got to say, you got it right, honey. I was one happy, happy soul who knew how to enjoy life to the fullest. Eating, drinking, cooking—oh, honey, those were my specialties! I was always into everything, a little of this, a little of that. I never stayed still too long. I had to be on the go, doing things and meeting new people. Your momma still makes me laugh, even from up here. She fusses at you every time you move because you always get rid of your old furniture to only buy new furniture. You know what her common line is, "You're just like Trudy, always getting new furniture every time you move". Tell her girl, we love living in the new. We may be broke rubbing two dimes together to make a dollar and all, but we looked and lived nice. Thank goodness you have a sense of financial maturity now.

People used to enjoy my company and taking care of me. It was a two-way street. See, what those did not know was if they opened up their eyes, they could see I was a true caregiver. I mean, how could I avoid it? My parents were Percy and Margaret, two people who have received recognition from multiple Presidents of the United States for taking care of children.

Believe me when I tell you their apples did not fall too far from the tree. As partners to our mates, it is only natural to ensure they have everything they need, which includes nourishment, love, companionship, security, and understanding. I've heard your husband Roger say that all he needs to get by is lovin and fried chicken. He has a point and if you look at it; he has only summed up what I've always shown you and my daughter, Cheryl. Love, love one another and others. When you love, everything will come naturally.

Now, let's talk about my girl, Cheryl. She's like a little slice of me, bless her heart. You two were tighter than two coats of paint growing up. While I was out there, living' it up and painting the town red, Cheryl was holding' down the fort with her grandma Margaret. I say that girls got a heart of gold, just like her grandma. I really appreciate your parents for letting you spend time with Cheryl as much as you did. I really liked that you and Cheryl always came to see me at a moment's notice. When I lived in both New Jersey and Virginia Beach, it seemed like the two of you always knew when to visit. Despite the distance not being a concern to you, you would drive, and I knew I could rely on you to bring Cheryl and my son Lionel to me. Y'all are grown now, but you are close like sisters, and I love that.

When away from home, oh, the adventures I had! I was a traveler, always ready to hit the road and to see what the world offered. No little old town was going to hold me back, not even the one I was born and raised in. Like me, you are not shy of a little adventure. That's right, girl, continue to take your journey and move around to see all that you can. Time waits for no one and if you have the opportunity, dive in and take up those opportunities for new experiences. I feel that is the connection between you and me. Our love was something different. It was like we had a bond that couldn't be broken by time or space. I guess it goes back to me pinching you when you were a baby to hear your little cry. But I guess you paid me back when you got older. During your training to become a hairdresser, do you remember that time you accidentally burned me in the middle of my back, with that dang curling iron? I ain't going to lie, it hurt like heck, but I rocked that scar with pride. A minor battle wound from the beauty frontline; you could say!

And my potato salad, honey! Lord, you and everyone have tried to crack the code, but it turns out, I took the recipe with me to the afterlife. It's my little secret up here, and I'm keeping' the heavens guessing as well. But watching you try to recreate it down there sure brought a smile to my face. I was laughing' with you, believe me.

Now, let's talk about that Roger of yours. That man's got a heart of gold, just like you. I heard he tried to make it to my sendoff but got himself lost along the way. Isn't that just like a good man, to show up for his friends in a time of sorrow, bless his heart? And speaking of hearts, I can tell he's got a big one, and I'm rooting for you two from up here. I know from experience that marriage can be tough. Believe me, I tried three times. Marriage takes God, love, patience, and humility. Keep that love alive and keep working towards winning regardless of the obstacles.

Truth be told, I am always praying for the women in our immediate family. Like you, I love companionship, whether it is temporary or long-term. I believe there is someone out there for everyone, but it takes work to make it work and it takes wearing blockers to defend the relationship from outside judgment and interference.

I know you miss me, sweet girl, and let me tell you, I miss you all, too. I miss our laughs, our jokes, and the way we would run the road speeding in cars with our lead feet to get to wherever we needed to go. You were my investigative partner in crime, my good troublemaker, and my source of endless laughs. And let's not forget our talks about men with ugly shoes and big water bucket heads—oh, the fun we had!

So, my dear, keep that spirit of ours alive. Keep laughing', keep Lovin', and keep showing the world that sass and spirit that runs deep in our blood. I may be up here, but I'm right there with you, every step of the way. And when you're ready to whip up another batch of that potato salad, just remember, I'm here watching, smiling', and maybe even giving you a little nudge in the right direction.

Sending you all my love and sass from up above,

Aunt Trudy

DEAR FREDDI

A Nod to Aunt Trudy's Potato Salad

This is not my exact recipe, but it is delicious enough to share at the next family cookout.

Ingredients:

4 cups diced and cooked potatoes (about 4-5 medium potatoes)

1/2 cup chopped celery

1/4 cup chopped yellow onion

1 cup mayonnaise

3 tablespoons Dijon mustard

2 tablespoons apple cider vinegar

2 teaspoon sugar

1 teaspoon salt (adjust to taste)

1/4 teaspoon black pepper (adjust to taste)

1/2 cayenne red pepper (adjust to taste)

Paprika, for garnish

Instructions:

1. Wash and scrub the potatoes. Cut them into bite size cubes.

2. Place the potato cubes in a pot of cold salted water. Bring to a boil over medium-high heat and cook until the potatoes are tender when pierced with a fork, about 10-15 minutes. Be careful not to overcook.

3. Drain and let cool.

4. In a mixing bowl, whisk together the mayonnaise, Dijon mustard, apple cider vinegar, lemon juice, sugar, salt, and black pepper until well combined. Adjust the seasonings to taste.

5. In a large mixing bowl, combine the cooked and cooled potato cubes, chopped celery, chopped red onion, and chopped parsley. Pour the dressing over the potato mixture.

6. Gently toss until the potatoes are well coated with the dressing.

7. Service potato salad warm or cover the potato salad and refrigerate for at least 12 hours, allowing the flavors to meld together.

DEAR FREDDI

CHAPTER 6: A LETTER FROM AUNT ALFREDA

Dear Freddi,

How are you and my girl Raya doing? I was looking down on you recently, seeing you compare the two pictures of me. One of you and me and the other of me and your daughter Raya. Yes, the similarities were the same. I was watching down praying on her just as I did over you. I vividly recall seeing you for the first time at your grandma Lizzy's house. Her house always seemed like home when we visited. I can still see the burgundy and gold printed wallpaper and green leather recliner chair and feel the closeness of all of your mom's family looking to get a glimpse of you. That day you came home from the hospital; you were all covered up with the receiving blanket. You looked just like your daddy with a little spiked mohawk.

You and Raya, y'all have the prettiest big legs. I always wished I had legs that were big to the bottom, like yours. Anyway, I hope this letter finds you with a heart full of love and a smile that warms even the brightest corner of Florida.

Can you believe you are releasing another book? I remember that day when you released your first book like it was yesterday, my dear. The excitement in the air and I was right there looking down from heaven, cheering you on with all the pride a heart can hold. You did it, and I couldn't be prouder. As I gaze down from the heavens, I see the path you've walked and the journey you've embraced. It warms my heart to see you flourishing, not afraid of anything, just as I knew you would. You've always had that bad ass fire within you, that drive to shine your light on the world. Your words, your stories, they're like a light of hope, reaching out to touch the hearts of those who read them. Keep on writing, girl, for your words and voice are a gifts that can change lives.

You know, I can't help but chuckle when I think about how folks used to think I was mean. Me, mean? Can you imagine? Well, I guess being a schoolteacher and a bus driver had its way of making folks believe I was tough as nails. But you and I know the truth, don't we? Beneath that exterior was a heart bursting with love, a heart that found its greatest joy in dancing, playing cards, and sharing meals with loved ones.

Speaking of meals, I can still taste those dishes we whipped up together in the kitchen during the holidays, like that stuffed ham a few years ago. Did you ever get my deviled egg recipe down? You know we did not write anything, so I hope you got it girl! You made the best cookies.

I loved it when the holidays rolled around because I could always count on you to bring me a big tin can filled with your delicious oatmeal raisin cookies. You made the old-fashioned kind that was so soft in the middle. Daddy preferred his hard, but you knew just how to make them for me. That sweet potato cake you make during Thanksgiving is also my favorite.

There are times like our family get-together that used to bring me so much happiness. I loved hearing you all having a good time but you know I never had a problem telling y'all to quiet down when the noise got too loud. Oh, the laughter and chatter that filled the air as we all got together, talking about town gossip, and sharing stories and food secrets.

Let's not forget to reminisce about those mischievous escapades you and my youngest son, Ryan, used to go on. Y'all were trouble, but it was only the two of you living on the ranch, so we all knew whatever trouble you got into, you were safe. Never until I watched you two had I seen two kids who were tasked with cutting grass turn lawnmowers into race cars. The two of you would drag racing through our yards on lawnmowers up and down the yards. Only you too could find stuff to get into like that.

Tori and I would get so mad when we would look out of our windows, towards the woody areas behind our homes, to see you and Ryan playing in the old, abandoned cars in the woods. God has always been on our side, as you two never got hurt from any of your escapades.

Sometimes I would go out to look for you two and you would be under the cars with your fathers trying your best to lend a hand to fix whatever was going on. You two thought you were race car drivers, and you were learning what needed to be done to fix your make believe cars. Kids today do not know how to have fun and play the way you and Ryan did. At the end of each day, we chased you and Ryan to the bathrooms to bathe before dinner. The both of you smelled like outside. Rain, snow or sunshine, you two made a way to have fun and enjoy yourselves.

Remember those bus rides? My, oh my, we sure owned those roads, didn't we? With you sitting behind me as my co-pilot, was always a joy. I cherished every moment we spent together as you helped me with the special needs children. You helped ensure that the children were cared for and assisted my bus aide in meeting their needs during their daily bus ride to and from school. I guess that is why it did not surprise me when I saw you in the process of opening an organization to help people with special needs. It is in your heart to help others and we are all up here praying and rooting you on through your journey towards success.

Kitty, my only daughter, and your god sister, she's a burst of sunshine mixed with a little trouble, just like you. I know you're watching out for her, even from afar, just as you promised me. You won't be in her business breathing down her neck, but you will be there if she needs to call, and I thank you for that.

Before passed away, I had a heart-to-heart with you and Roger. I asked you to look after Kitty, to be her support and her guide after her daddy and I left life on earth. I knew that even though miles might separate you, your bond is unbreakable, and I appreciate you only wanting the best for her. Thank you for also lending your parents to help Kitty. My brother is a great man and Torie is that force that won't let anything bad happen to my children as she sees them as her own. That's love!

Times will get tough and memories from the past will creep in and make you want to wander but stay strong and remember the Daily Bread. It was my favorite source of inspiration. God will lead you. Until we meet again, dance on tabletops, cook with love, lead with pride, love your neighbors, pray daily, and know that you are cherished.

With all my love,
Aunt Alfreda

DEAR FREDDI

Brunch Deviled Eggs Recipe

Eggs and bacon what a wonderful combination. Here is a spin on the duo in this deviled egg recipe. Try serving this at the next family brunch.

Ingredients:

6 large eggs

2 tablespoons mayonnaise

1 teaspoon Dijon mustard

2 teaspoon sweet relish

1 teaspoon cider vinegar

Salt and pepper to taste

Paprika, for garnish

Crumbled bacon for garnish

Instructions:

1. Place the eggs and a pinch of salt in a single layer in a saucepan and cover them with about an inch of water. Bring the water to a rolling boil over medium-high heat.

2. Once boiling, cover the saucepan and remove it from the heat. Let the eggs sit in the hot water for about 9-15 minutes, depending on the desired yolk consistency.

3. Drain the hot water and transfer the eggs to a bowl of ice water to cool. Let them sit for a few minutes before peeling.

4. Once the eggs are cooled and peeled, slice them in half lengthwise. Gently remove the yolks and place them in a mixing bowl.

5. Mash the yolks with a fork until smooth and crumbly.

6. Add mayonnaise, Dijon mustard, sweet relish, white vinegar, salt, and black pepper to the yolks.

7. Using hand mixer whip until all ingredients are combined, and the mixture is creamy and fluffy.

8. Fill the Eggs:

9. If you want to pipe the filling into the eggs, you can use a piping bag or a plastic sandwich bag with a corner snipped off. Alternatively, you can simply spoon the filling into the egg halves.

10. Carefully spoon or pipe the yolk mixture into the egg white halves.

11. Garnish and Serve:

12. Crumble bacon over eggs

13. Sprinkle paprika over the top of each deviled egg for added color and flavor.

14. Place the deviled eggs on a serving platter or plate. Cover and refrigerate until ready to serve.

15.

DEAR FREDDI

CHAPTER 7: A LETTER FROM MARTIN

Dear Freddi,

Girl, I've been following you and your journey, you jive turkey you. I sit here smiling from ear to ear with my heart full of love and gratitude. Can you believe it's been three years since I departed life on earth? COVID-19 took me and others out in such a short time. Time sure does fly, doesn't it? Friend, I want you to know that all I can remember are good times and laughter when I think of our friendship. Remember those good old high school days? You were shy and stayed away from us upperclassmen, but out of school, you and your girls were the life of the party. I swore y'all had the cleanest cars for girls in the entire county. I also had respect for you. You and your crew never looked to use a person. Although you were in school, you worked and made your own money. Whenever you and I cross paths, we always share laughs, dreams, and some of the best times of our lives. I talked about the up-and-down relationships I had, and you would do the same.

Life took us down different paths and we ended up living on opposite sides of the country, but you and I, we always stayed connected. I'll never forget those times I'd call just to check in and give you a hard time, calling you a jive turkey and asking what you were up to. And oh, washing your car when you came home to visit that was my way of showing you that even from afar, I was right there by your side, looking out for you.

You know, they say opposites attract, and that couldn't have been truer for us. A big homegrown guy like me and a spirited, outgoing traveling soul like you, we would have made quite the pair. Behind my tough exterior, I was just a big old teddy bear, and you, well, you were the spark that brought out the best in me. The best part of our friendship was it never ended.

Live music and concerts. Now that was our bond, wasn't it? The energy, the vibes, hearing, and being in the presence of it was like magic. I'll never forget that weekend I drove up to Philly to visit you and went to see Jamie Foxx in concert. The way he blended music and comedy was pure genius. And oh, every time Gerald LeVert came to town, we would go together so we could see him wowing the crowd that left us in awe. He had a way of performing, just like his daddy. Our love for music was a bond that couldn't be broken, and those memories still bring a smile to my face.

Our paths may have diverged, but our friendship remained real. Even when you moved on to your new chapter with Roger, I kept checking up on you. I remember one call, which left me feeling a little sad. One day when going down to the carwash I passed your parents' house and saw your car. I called you to meet me down at the carwash and you flew into me. You told me you were about to get married and that you did not need to meet me anywhere. You were mad but you know it were not my intention to disrespect you, our Roger. A little bird told me during that time that you were being a Bridezilla, all stressed about your wedding and treating everyone mean. I laugh now, but then my little feelings were hurt. From that day on I held my distance but did still check up on you. Except for that one call, I looked forward to all our calls. Those phone calls, these laughter-filled chats where we caught up on the small-town gossip and shared the latest happenings. They were the highlights of my days.

You were more than just a friend; you were a kindred spirit. We might have called ourselves Fairweather friends, but our connection was anything but fleeing. Remember our theme song, "Fairweather Friend" by Johnny Gill? Those lyrics captured the essence of our friendship perfectly. Through thick and thin, rain or shine, we stood by each other's side, sharing laughter and stories that time could never erase.

As I look down from above, I want you to let you know how proud I am of the person you've become. Your spirit, your determination, it shines as brightly as ever. Keep on sharing new experiences with those around you, keep dancing to the rhythm of life, keep on sharing your stories with the world, and keep on being that radiant soul that can light up a room.

Whenever you hear a song that makes your heart dance and you feel a gentle breeze against your skin, know that I'm right there with you, cheering you on. Our friendship might be different now, but the love we shared is still as strong as ever. Until we meet again on the other side, my friend keeps shining, keeps laughing, and keeps sharing the magic that is uniquely you.

With love and laughter,

Martin

Philly Cheese Steak Sandwich

This is a great hit when having family and friends over to watch the big game.

Ingredients:

For the Steak:

 1 pound thinly sliced ribeye steak

 Salt and pepper, to taste

 2 tablespoons vegetable oil

 1 medium thinly sliced onion

For the Sandwich:

 4 hoagie rolls or sub rolls

 6 slices provolone cheese

2 tablespoons butter

 Salt and pepper, to taste

 Lettuce leaves

 Sliced tomatoes

 Mayonnaise

Instructions:

1. Heat a large skillet over medium-high heat. Add the vegetable oil.
2. Season the thinly sliced ribeye steak with salt and pepper.

3. Add the steak slices to the skillet and cook for about 2-3 minutes on each side until browned and cooked to your desired level of doneness. Remove from the skillet and set aside.

4. In the same skillet, melt the butter over medium heat.

5. Add the thinly sliced onions. Cook, stirring occasionally, until the onions are caramelized and slightly charred. Season with salt and pepper to taste.

6. Preheat the oven to 350°F (175°C).

7. Split the hoagie rolls open and place them on a baking sheet, layering each roll with slices of the cooked steak.

8. Top the steak with a generous number of sauteed onions.

9. Lay slices of provolone cheese over the onions.

10. Place the baking sheet in the preheated oven and bake for about 5 minutes, or until the cheese is melted and bubbly.

11. Remove the baking sheet from the oven.

12. Layer lettuce leaves and sliced tomatoes on top of the melted cheese.

13. Spread Mayo and Serve

DEAR FREDDI

CHAPTER 8: A LETTER FROM COOLCAT

Dear Freddi,

Hey, how's it going, Goddaughter? I can't stop thinking about your baptism day, it's so special to me. Time flies, it's crazy. I remember that day like it was yesterday. Your Auntie Juanita and I were so proud to accept you as our goddaughter in front of everyone we love. It was a truly amazing and special moment that I'll never forget. On that day, I promised to always look out for you, and I still am from up here.

Aunt Juanita rocked her pink printed blouse and rose-colored pants, proving her grace and style. Well, Cool would not be a part of my name if I weren't representing the cool godfather, Coolcat. I was stylin' in my dark blue shirt and white pants, wearing a gold linked bracelet and shades.

One thing that made that day so great was when we gave you a small charm bracelet as a symbol of our bond. It was a sweet way of showing you how much I care. You, my goddaughter, looked so cute in your little white dress and matching hat. Everyone laughed joyfully as the help kept sliding off of your little head.

Can I tell you that I am still honored that your incredible momma and daddy, thought that much of me, to want me to be your godfather?

Your mom, Tori, was like one of my favorite cousins. At some point, she's been the boss of all of us. Torie's love for her family will leave a lasting impact on all of us up here and still living down there with you. Praying you'll keep the family legacy going. I see you have distanced yourself from the family, but I'm hoping you will find your way back. There's no such thing as perfect people or perfect families. Life's not always fair and families fight, but we're all family, so remember that.

You know I used to smoke. Smoking is no joke - it can seriously mess up your health. I'm happy you kicked the smoking habit. There's so much more to life, trust me. I wish I had more time. I missed out on a ton of magical moments, like dancing with Marcy at her wedding. I saw from up above that she was the most gorgeous bride ever, but I couldn't be there in the flesh. I'm always up here humming the melody to "Dance with My Father". She was stunning. She's my girl and I'll love her forever, even in eternity.

The big guy up here has his own plans, and everything depends on his timing. But sometimes I think, if technology and research were as advanced as they are now in your time, maybe I could have lived longer on earth. On the flip side, the big guy never messes up and life is amazing in his promised land. I wish I could scream from here to everyone who smokes. Please stop that habit right now! Let's make it a thing of the past. Tell everyone not to miss out on the magical moment and quit smoking.

I've seen that throughout your life, you have offered support and discreet direction to people going through life's difficulties. Your work as a motivational coach makes us confident that you'll carry on your family's tradition of offering support to those in need. You're there to help, not harm, and you're really straightforward about telling people when they need more support than you can offer. Watching you grow into a strong woman is a beautiful reminder of Aunt Eula and our family's love and commitment.

I want to share some of the coolest advice you'll probably ever hear, as you keep on living your life. You're an amazing role model. Your great aunt Eula taught some valuable lessons to children. I hope you and your family will never forget them.

Spread that love that never gives up: It's the type of love that has no limits, no flaws, and is always by your side, no matter what. Embrace this love and let it lead how you interact with your hubby and kids. Love them with all your heart, just like God loves you. Hang in there: life's tough, but just remember to stay strong when your patience is tested. When facing challenges, just take a deep breath and try to be patient with others. You're like a rock to others, always providing guidance and support to them. Be the rock for your family, always there to listen, give honest advice, and support them in everything they do. Continue to cherish every moment with your family. Continue to create beautiful memories together and let those moments become the foundation of a loving and strong bond.

I have no doubt that you will continue to be an incredible person, just as your parents. Your husband and children are lucky to have you in their lives. I know that you will fill their life with love and cherished memories.

As your godfather, I am always here looking over you from the coolest place ever to support and guide you toward greatness. I may not be physically present, but my love and blessings are always with you. Please remember that your eternal family has lined up and are here to support you in this beautiful journey of life.

With all my love and blessings,
Coolcat

Coolcat's Smooth and Creamy Banana Pudding Recipe

This banana is just as smooth and silky as me. Make this a tasty treat to eat anytime during the year.

Ingredients:

1 cup raw cane or granulated sugar

1/3 cup all-purpose flour

1/4 teaspoon salt

3 large egg yolks

2 cups whole milk

1 teaspoon pure vanilla extract

5 ripe bananas, sliced

1 box (about 12 ounces) vanilla wafer cookies

Instructions:

1. In a medium-sized saucepan, whisk together the sugar, flour, and salt. In a separate bowl, beat the egg yolks with the milk until well combined.

2. Gradually whisk the egg yolk mixture into the dry ingredients in the saucepan. Place the saucepan over medium heat and cook, stirring constantly, until the mixture thickens. This should take about 10-15 minutes. You want the pudding to coat the back of a spoon.

3. Remove the saucepan from the heat and stir in the vanilla extract. Let the pudding cool slightly.

4. In a trifle dish or a large glass bowl, layer the bottom with a third of the vanilla wafers. Top with half of the sliced bananas. Pour half of the warm pudding over the bananas and spread it out evenly.

5. Add another layer of vanilla wafers, the remaining sliced bananas, and the rest of the pudding.

6. Refrigerate the banana pudding for at least 4 hours, or overnight, to allow the flavors to meld and the pudding to set.

7. Serve chilled and enjoy your delicious creamy banana pudding!

DEAR FREDDI

CHAPTER 9: A LETTER FROM CHARLOTTE

Hi Freddi,

When I began writing this letter, I thought I had plenty of time to prepare my letter for your upcoming book of a future installment within the book series. However, God had other plans for me. Please know I heard your prayers. I felt your love asking God to heal my physical limitations. God decided it was time for me to be released from life on earth to live a pain-free, mobile eternal life in his heavens.

I am in a better place. I'm with my momma and I am happy no longer feeling pain. You never met momma, but she sees you and Roger. I told her that whenever I asked Roger how you were, he would say, "she still crazy". Momma laughed so hard because she saw him telling you the same thing about me. Momma says she sees you and Roger both being crazy and happy together.

I really enjoyed our conversations, laughter, and the moments we shared when you visited. Although we only got to know one another over a short span of time, I loved and appreciated how you helped my brother. Roger was one of the blessed ones, as he was able to be blessed with true love twice in a lifetime, and I know that was God's work. Please know that although my physical presence is no longer with you, please know that my spirit continues to radiate joy, love, and affection towards you.

Before passing away, I found myself thinking about the good times we spent together during your visits to Carolina and even during phone conversations. That time means a lot to me. I looked forward to speaking to you and Roger on the phone because you were always on the move going somewhere, even if it were somewhere close like to the store. Roger would talk on and on that about 30 minutes into the conversation he would say, "Charlotte, Freddi's here". I never understood why you didn't say anything, but when you said you loved him for giving his siblings alone time, it made sense. You never meant to take away Roger's family time. I could tell that a family, especially a loving and supportive one, means a lot to you. Now, once you spoke up and you and I began talking, it was like Roger was nowhere present. It tickled me when you would say Roger is the baby boy and I'm the baby girl. I can't tell you why it was funny to me, but it always made both you and I laugh. I guess looking at ourselves in our 50s as babies was funny.

Oh, I will not let this time go by without mentioning our shared love for good fried chicken and the delightful greasy indulgences from the Cookout fast-food restaurant! I think we can both shamelessly admit that our ankles didn't appreciate all the salt, but we savored every bite as if it were a rare delicacy. Those moments of guilty pleasure are etched in my heart, a reminder of the simple joys in life that we must embrace. Remember, we bonded over love, a chicken drumstick for me, and a wing for you. How funny is that?

One thing that always struck me about you was your mission to visit family regardless of the distance. I could tell it was you because Roger did not do pop-ups. It was like you would call and then suddenly appear. I Remember you calling out of the blue say hey Charlotte, what are you doing for Easter, then popping up at my door visiting me. That is what I cherish about my family. They made sure I had the love and support I needed when I could no longer physically do for myself.

Sister-in-law, I want you to know that I have been watching over you all from here. While I may not be able to touch your hand or share a laugh in person, I am with you in spirit, smiling over you and singing, as Roger would say, referring to the whine in my voice. Something else you and I have in common. Please continue to comfort Roger, knowing I am at peace, and I want nothing more than for you to live in happiness and joy in your life. You see, my journey through life, despite its challenges, has taught me the power of faith and resilience. Even in my silence, I hope to have inspired you to find strength in the face of adversity, to remain hopeful when faced with uncertainty, and to keep your heart open to the beauty of life.

Always remember that the Lord's work is boundless, and his ability to make the impossible possible and knows no limits. My faith in him was unshakable, and I want you to hold on to that faith as well. Through prayer, belief, and love, you will find the strength to overcome any obstacle that comes your way.

As I look down upon you and our family, I am grateful. Grateful for the love we shared, grateful for the memories that continue to warm my heart, and grateful for the love and care you gave me during my time on earth. Please remember to cherish every moment, savor every meal, and find joy in the simple pleasures of life. I will always be in your heart, a guardian angel watching over you.

With all my love and the warmest of smiles,

Charlotte

Charlotte's Creamy Mashed Potatoes and Gravy

This is a great side dish to go with just about every meal

Ingredients:

4 large russet potatoes, peeled and diced into 1 inch chunks

6 tablespoons unsalted butter

1/2 cup 2% reduced fat milk, warmed

Salt and pepper to taste

Chopped fresh chives or parsley for garnish (optional)

Instructions:

1. Place the diced potatoes in a large pot and cover them with cold water. Add a pinch of salt to the water.

2. Bring the water to a boil over high heat, then reduce the heat to medium and simmer, until the potatoes are tender and can be easily pierced with a fork.

3. Drain the potatoes in a colander and return them to the pot.

4. Add the butter to the potatoes and mash them with a potato masher until the butter is melted, and the potatoes are mostly smooth.

5. Pour in the warm milk and continue mashing until the potatoes are creamy. You can add more milk if needed to reach your desired consistency.

6. Season the mashed potatoes with salt and pepper to taste. Be sure to taste it as you go to get the seasoning just right.

7. In a bowl pour gravy then add a layer of mashed potato, then
    repeat with gravy. If like, garnish with chopped fresh chives or
    parsley for a burst of color and freshness.

Gravy Recipe:

Ingredients:

 2 tablespoons butter

 2 tablespoons all-purpose flour

 1 cup chicken or beef broth

 1/2 cup 2% reduced fat milk

 Salt and pepper to taste

Instructions:

1. In a medium-sized saucepan, melt the butter over medium
    heat.
2. Once the butter is melted and bubbling slightly, add the flour.
    Stir continuously with a whisk to create a smooth roux (a
    pastel-like mixture). Cook the roux for 12 minutes to remove
    the raw flour taste but be careful not to let it brown.
3. Gradually whisk in the chicken or beef broth, ensuring there
    are no lumps. Continue to whisk until the mixture thickens,
    which should take about 35 minutes.
4. Slowly pour in the milk while whisking constantly. Continue
    to cook and whisk until the gravy thickens and reaches your
    desired consistency. This may take an added 23 minutes.

5. Season the gravy with salt and pepper to taste. Remember that you can always add more, so start with a little and adjust as needed.

6. Remove the gravy from the heat.

DEAR FREDDI

CHAPTER 10: A LETTER FROM RAMONA

Dear Freddi,

Hi, I never met you, but I see you! Just so you know, love knows no limits! I'm saying this because we never crossed paths before, but now that I see you and my son adores you, so I love you. I've noticed Roger sharing stories about us with you. I know you through watching your friendship and love story with Roger.

It brings me great joy to see this life that you and Roger have built out of tragedy, a bond that reminds me of the love I shared with my son. My son is speaking the truth when he says there is no love greater than mine, but I see and know you truly love him, and I appreciate that because you have truly loved him through good and tough times. I may not be physically present, but I watch over you both with a heart full of love and pride. Through your journey, I've seen how you've become a major part of each other's lives, and I want to share some heartfelt words of wisdom, humor, and encouragement with you.

While raising Roger and his siblings, I found myself navigating the challenges of life with a sense of humor and determination. Just like you, I was a woman that loved to travel and enjoyed exploring new places, with the Bahamas being one of my favorite destinations. I can see that you share this passion for travel, and I hope that you and

Roger continue to create beautiful memories together, just as I did with my son.

Some of my best memories are from moments in the kitchen cooking for my family. I loved making fried pork chops for Roger and sending him down to the local Chinese carryout for the best gravy in town. See my smothered pork chops were not completed without the gravy. Oh, how I would laugh to myself when he returned, because although he is a slim guy, he will go on a mission to satisfy his's culinary cravings.

He is the youngest of his siblings and the one who spent the longest time in the house with me. I remember his mischievous grin when he would return from driving my little Honda Civic, and I would arrange the miniature figures on the dashboard to let him know I was watching over his speed. It was funny to me because he never knew how I knew he was speeding. See, I knew because of how my figurines on the dash shifted. They only shifted when you drove above a certain speed or slammed on brakes. Later I found out he got hip to the game and would remove all the figurines, place them in a box then re-arrange them upon his return from errands.

You know, I had a unique sense of smell that couldn't tolerate most perfumes. Your dear husband, always the thoughtful son, would gift me tiger-printed items instead of pretty flowers and perfumes. It warms my heart to know that you share this connection through your admiration for animal prints which are symbols of strength and resilience.

When talking with Roger, I always encouraged him to be his real self and not be afraid to show passion about work, love and life. I saw his potential, just as I see yours. I introduced him to the world of office work, sending him to typewriter class, which eventually paved the way for his career and your own friendship. He loved dressing up in those suits and wearing ties. I always saved magazines for him so he could see the latest styles for men. When he began working for the law offices in downtown Alexandria, Virginia, he could not wait to take his paycheck to Cavilar Men Shop, in Tyson's Corner, to buy his suits. It's incredible to think that my small act played a part in the beautiful love story you two have created.

As you navigate this journey with Roger, I want you to remember that patience and understanding are key. My son may take his time processing things, but it's in those moments that he truly absorbs and appreciates life. He's a simple man at heart, with a love for family and commitment to those he cares about.

From here I've witnessed the moments when you find yourself being hard on Roger and easily frustrated with his actions or non-actions. I want to gently remind you to let go of the stuff you can't change and embrace the laughter that you both share. I really understand the major things that need to be dealt with can't be let go. Yes you may need to push my son to get things resolved but the little stuff, don't sweat it, things will work out. I see you pushing to make him more accountable, which I understand. No one knows when God will call them to eternal life, and you are trying to prepare Roger if you pass but ease up as these things tend to work themselves out. You know I've been giving you little signs. I'll playfully rattle a picture frame or two to remind you and Roger to lighten up and focus on the joy that fills your home. I've seen you two during those moments of heated fellowship and I don't like it. Both of you argue over meaningless things. It is going to be okay, enjoy your time together. Love one another and forgive one another for past actions, and past words, because it won't matter if either of you is gone tomorrow. Best friends are what you entered this relationship as, so remember best friends are what you will always be.

Laughter, my dear, is the medicine that can mend any wound, bridge any gap, and nurture the love that binds you and Roger together. Embrace the quirks, celebrate the shared moments, and cherish the unique connection you both hold.

As I watch over you and Roger, I am filled with pride and happiness. You have my blessing, and I am grateful to have you as a part of my extended family. Your love story is different, and it shows the power of connecting with good people that are sent to us.

Enjoy every day like it was your last,

Ramona

DEAR FREDDI

DMV Fried Chops

Ingredients:

For the Pork Chops:

4 bone-in pork chops

Salt and pepper, to taste

Peanut oil, for frying

1 cup all-purpose flour

2 tablespoons Old Bay seasoning

1 teaspoon paprika

1 teaspoon garlic powder

1 teaspoon onion powder

1 teaspoon cayenne pepper (adjust to taste)

Instructions:

1. Pat the pork chops dry with paper towels. Season both sides with salt and pepper.

2. In a shallow dish or plastic bag, combine the flour, Old Bay seasoning, paprika, garlic powder, onion powder, and cayenne pepper. Mix well to create the dry mixture.

3. One at a time, coat each pork chop in the Old Bay dry mixture, pressing the mixture onto the meat to adhere. Shake off any excess.

4. In a large skillet, heat about 1/2 inch of peanut oil over medium high heat until it reaches 350°F (175°C).

5. Carefully place the coated pork chops in the hot oil. Fry for about 8 minutes on each side, or until they are golden brown and cooked through. The internal temperature of the pork chops should reach 145°F (63°C).

6. Use tongs to carefully remove the fried pork chops from the skillet and place them on a plate lined with paper towels to drain excess oil.

7. Let the fried pork chops rest for a few minutes before serving.

DEAR FREDDI

CHAPTER 11: A LETTER FROM REGINALD

Dear Freddi,

Can you believe we're meeting like this? Listen up, I gotta tell you something. Even though I'm up here with the Big Guy, I'm one of his angels who's still got some earthy hood in 'em. I'm a bit different from your typical guardian angel, but I know you're different too, so you can relate. You gotta remember, not everything or everyone fits into a neat little box. I know you had a lot of questions about me, and it's been tough for my son to answer because honestly, I wasn't around much. Ramona, Roger's mom, and I broke up when he was about to start high school. It was tough because I didn't wanna leave her and the kids, but I had stuff going on. I knew Ramona would be alright 'cause she had that fire in her and she was gonna make things happen.

When I met Ramona, she had four girls and was doing it all on her own. They were such a pretty little family. It wasn't easy to impress Ramona, who always looked great. She made sure our connection was strong before we started dating and bringing me around her girls. As time went by, Ramona and I started to have more children. We had three boys, the youngest being your husband, Roger.

I've been watching Roger from up here for a while and I've realized I should've spent more time with him, but I did what I could back then. My dad died when I was young, so I had no clue how to be a dad. I just figured it out as I went along. I messed up. I only focused on making Roger a great athlete, not realizing that football wasn't his thing. His mom saw his real skills - reading and writing. Sometimes I was a good husband, sometimes not so much. Roger was right there, watching me take care of our home and make sure everything was good. People knew better than to mess with me, Ramona, and the kids. We worked hard every day to take care of our family.

The night Roger got shot, I went out to find those punks and took care of business. Looking back, I shouldn't have retaliated, but those punks deserved it. Those kids were going around robbing people in the neighborhood as they got home from work. My boy was finishing his shift at Safeway and as soon as he got off the bus, these punks tried to rob Roger, asking him to give up his kicks and dough. Roger noticed one of the punks, so they thought it would be best to shoot him and make a run for it. Those young folks didn't have a clue about shooting a gun, thankfully, because the bullet went right through Roger's leg. He was on crutches for a bit but trust me, I handled it.

So, after your wedding, Renee told you all about the time she got jumped. And I made her go back to the neighborhood where it happened to fight everyone who laid a hand on her that day. The thing is, we weren't gonna let anyone disrespect us. What's messed up is that Renee's so-called friend, Rosalind Banks, was one of the girls who fought her.

Renee's story that day is the same as what went down between you and Chipper. Ramona and I have never had a situation like you and Roger, so I get that things are different. Chipper is not on board with you and Roger being happy. If I could have been there, I would have had your back when Chipper disrespected you. Chipper knew you and Roger were close before getting married, and I don't think Chipper liked you were that close to Roger. Chipper was well aware that Roger shared stories with you about his exes, so it made me want to come down there from these pearly gates to rattle some things around when Chipper came to your wedding with Roger's ex-girlfriend, Tyra. Chipper looks to be a real chump. Thank the lord you have all of us up here praying for your family and marriage.

There are folks out there who thrive on relationship drama, so stay strong and keep those bad vibes away. You're a total powerhouse. I see you fighting battles for your family that Roger doesn't see. Make sure you take care of yourself while fighting those battles. I know you're on some medicine for your blood pressure. Keep taking your medicine as the doctor told you. Roger told you I passed away because of a stroke. I wasn't taking my medicine like I should have, even though Ramona nagged me to take the stuff that was supposed to keep me alive. I didn't listen and died young. I used to feel so good and full of energy that I didn't think I needed the medicine. But now I'm all set and ready to make a difference up here. I'm really proud of my children. Roger, the baby, always knows how to surprise our family. Thanks for having his back. Keep supporting Roger and pushing him to chase his dreams by giving him the support he needs. There are dream killers out there, but you're not one of them. You've pushed my son further than I ever could. Let me tell you, in my day I would have steered clear of someone like you, all smart and ambitious. Roger loves that, but I would've been scared of you because I couldn't keep up. Please keep doing what you're doing to push my son to new limits.

Peace & Respect,
Reginald

Cinnamon Fried Apples

This is one of my favorite dishes during the winter months that my kids hated. Fried apples were warm and tasty and reminded me of the time in the kitchen spent with my mother. I can hear her telling me Reginald doesn't let the apples stick to the pan. When she finished cooking them, we would eat the fried apples on toast or top of ice cream.

Ingredients:
1 tablespoon water

½ cup butter

¼ cup white sugar

¼ cup brown sugar

2 tablespoons ground cinnamon, or to taste

4 Granny Smith apples - peeled, cored, and sliced

Directions

1. Add water to the large skillet, then layer the pan with the sliced apples, topped with white sugar, brown sugar, butter, and cinnamon.
2. Occasionally stir sauteing apples over low heat until softened, 15 to 25 minutes.

DEAR FREDDI

CHAPTER 12: A LETTER FROM JERRY

Dear Freddi,

Our paths crossed in a way that none of us could have predicted. You were one of Roger's best friends, his confidante, his dude, and over time, you became so much more. During my time there on earth, I knew about your friendship and was very much okay with it. See on those morning drives to work, I would talk to my friend Melvin and Roger would talk to you or Sharon. That was our morning routine. The stories that Roger would tell me about you and Sharon's dating lives kept us on the floor laughing. You two single ladies were funny. See, I was a woman who knew who my husband's genuine friends were and understood their connection. Roger spent his teens and adult life around women. At home, he had 6 sisters, and he worked in an office environment. Women surrounded Roger for most of his life, which is why he has so many female friends. So sadly, by now I bet you have run into people who don't understand you being ok with Roger and his female friends. I'm here to tell you, don't let their thoughts and comments ruin your relationship.

So, the first time I met you at my 40th birthday party, remember me tip-toeing into the venue blindfolded thinking Roger had bought me a new suburban? Did I look surprised when he took off the blindfold? Girl, I hope I did because I think I kind of knew he was throwing me a party. So, in the beginning, I did not want to go all out to celebrate my 40th birthday, but then at the last minute, I told him it would be nice to do something. Whatever the case, he sure pulled it off, and I was so happy to see everyone. That was a fun evening. I danced to "Before I Let Go" with my 1st love, my daddy. Oh, how I love my daddy. When I heard the DJ play the first couple of notes from the song, I yelled across the room, "Daddy", and he met me on the dance floor, and we stepped. As a daddy's girl, you understand, my daddy meant the world to me, and I look over him and mamma as well. My family showed out and partied. After getting home, Roger and I laughed later that evening when opening gifts. He told me you kept texting him asking me not to open your card until last because there was no money in the card. Honey, it was the thought that counts and honestly, look at what you are doing for me now. You are helping raise my children, and that is significantly more than I could have asked for. I guess looking back, it was good that he had the 40th birthday party because I unexpectedly passed away 3 short years after the party, at 43.

Through Roger, you and I shared our laughs, even though our re-gifting surprises for others. Roger re-enacted the looks and expression on Sharon's face when he gave her the scented candle set on her 40th birthday. I wish I could have been there. Roger said, Sharon almost fainted and cried, saying, "Roger knows just what I like". Little did she know it was a gift for me he had bought, but the candles stunk. As

I mentioned, although you and I were not in direct contact with each other, we knew enough of each other that I can honestly say I had respect for you for being a loyal friend to Roger.

Remember that night when the four of us—me, Roger, Derrick and, you—went out for happy-hour, drinks, and laughs on a double date night at the Tiki Docks? For one, I was surprised when you and Derrick walked into the restaurant together. I did not know you and Derrick were dating each other. That night, although you and I did not have a relationship, we were very familiar with each other's stories because we had similar upbringings as Southern Maryland country girls. That night you guys poked fun at me, thinking one of the young men at the music event we attended was making a pass at me. I could see Derrick getting enraged and told the man, "That lady's husband is sitting right there". Then the man, who was smaller than Roger and Derrick, face whiter than the sand we were standing on, looks at you, and says I want her and pointed at you. Talk about funny. It was hilarious because Derrick said nothing, and you were his date. We teased Derrick all that night because he did not have a response to the man. I cherished those moments because we laughed and built a genuine connection. Later that night Roger and I couldn't help but laugh at your facial expressions towards Derrick. Being messy, Derrick stretched cheese from your nachos clear across the table, consuming every piece of your nachos, leaving strings of cheese everywhere. Girl, from that night on I knew you were alright. In my book, if you could put up with that, you showed you had all the patience in the world to deal with other bumps that came your way.

You were one of Roger's friends that I thought I would see and talk to again but, God had other plans for us. In the blink of an eye, I was gone, at 43 years young, just 9 months after our double date, leaving behind a world of memories and shattered dreams. I recall looking from above the disbelief in your eyes when Roger broke the news to you. He first sent you a text and told you I passed away. You thought he was lying, then he called you at work and said, Jerry passed". I saw how you rushed to the hospital from your job in Richmond, Virginia, racing against time and distance to be by his side. I saw true friendship. Your support and presence comforted him during those darkest hours, and in your shared grief, a bond grew stronger.

I'm not going to lie, Roger and I used to laugh watching that Seinfeld show episode when they spoke about those waiting in the wind. It is funny you were never a thought. I do laugh because you are his friend and you have been there all the time. Thank you but know we still talked about you and your crazy relationships. Roger told me about the many days he pulled you off of the ledge. Yeah, he told me about the night you had Raya in the car, trying to get that old man TJ's attention. Funny Raya brought you back to reality quick by saying, mommy, it's cold out here let's go home. Laugh because you know that was funny. You had the baby stalking old men with you, looking in the parking lot for his car and stuff. It is so funny to now laugh at the type of stuff we do as single, young, dumb women.

After my passing, God heard your prayers, as you cried asking God what was Roger going to do, how was he going to take care of his two children alone. God put you in a place to be that help Roger needed. Not an easy task but it was a promise you made on that fateful day–a promise to stand by Roger's side, as his friend, to help him navigate the turbulent waters of single parenthood, grief and loss. As I watch you both now, I see how that promise has blossomed into a love that is so unique that others can't understand. Your daughter, Roger and our children–our once awkward, unconventional family–have found comfort, companionship, and healing in one another. I look at our children, all three, and I still don't know if they know how blessed they are. So many people are praying for them. Everyone is rooting for them to win, and they are winning.

I'm up here in heaven, praying hard for you, Roger, and the kids. I know people have made things tough for you, and you didn't ask for any of this judgment, but I just want you to know that I appreciate you. It was so tough to imagine anyone else doing what you've done to help Roger and the kids have a somewhat normal life after my death. I know it has been a journey of tears, arguments, laughter, heartache, and healing. I want you to know that I am watching over you and doing my best to help you with my crew every step of the way.

Relationships can be tough, and I can see that blending this family hasn't been a breeze for you, especially since you had to become the disciplinary parent to my children. Blending two families looks to be one of the hardest things to do. I can see the struggles you guys face when trying to create one unit. I notice how you talk differently. You're so spontaneous, and you don't mind being by yourself. You're so different from the person that I was, and that's been a huge change for Roger and the kids. Rather than being open to adjustment, some find it simpler to avoid dealing with the change and create separation.

There was a time when Zack was bonding with you, but then things took a turn. It seemed like he was caught in the middle of bonding with you and Raya, or choosing to remain loyal to me and his sister. I prayed over my children and often prayed they would see that there was no harm in loving you and Raya. There is always room in the heart to love more people. Zack and Raya's connection was going well, but things got complicated when Tasha returned from her first year in college. She saw how close Zack and Raya had become while watching the two play video games together. Tasha entered the room where the kids were playing and demanded that Zack stop playing with Raya. Tasha shouted, "Raya will not take my place in this family", and Freddi will never replace Mommy". She continued, "I wish Freddi was dead instead of Mommy, I hate everything about her". Those words and that situation broke my heart because so much pain from my passing was taken out on you. As you know, Tasha is a great, loving, calm person. She was hurting inside and had no one but girlfriends from school to talk to. I saw Raya run up the stairs to her room to cry, you went up to check on her, and Roger sat there shocked. It was written all over his face. He couldn't wrap his head around the fact that his daughter despised you and Raya so much. He was speechless. After you checked on Raya, I saw you stand over Tasha, yelling at her, saying how things were harder for you because she looked so much like me. You told her at that moment you wanted to smack the taste out of her mouth, and you looked at Roger to step in. I saw Roger tell you he could not correct Tasha for her actions because, to him, he would be looking at me. At that moment, I wanted to hug all of you because everyone was reacting to hurt. Every one of you was dealing with grief. Tasha was reacting to missing her mommy. She missed her mom so much as she navigated through her teens and young adult stages of life. You were hurt because you wanted Roger to stand up for you. I needed my children, Raya, Roger, and you to know that you needed one another, the arguing and fighting had to stop. You cried and looked at everyone in the room and told them it was like she had a hold on Roger and Zack because she was the spitting image of me.

So much was said that day and all of you were impacted. Both you and Tasha had scars that ran deep for years and transcended into the relationships within the family. What I found to be sad was the input of other adults who fed into Tasha's rage instead of helping. During that time, I saw you looked as though you all wanted Roger to fix the situation, but he could not. That day led to tears for everyone.

After everything was said and done, Zack, never really spoke to you again and started avoiding Raya just as Tasha wanted. It broke my heart to see this and how much it hurt everyone. I see often the feeling from that day still lives in your heart and it's totally fine to feel the way you do, and it's okay to admit that you're hurt. It is never right for anyone to purposely hurt another person because they are in pain. The saying is right, hurt people, hurt people", and that was what all of you were doing.

Following that incident, I saw you have a much-needed talk with Roger about getting counseling for everyone. Family and individual counseling was needed because everyone had gone through so much. I felt relieved when he agreed to go to counseling and to also seek counseling for the children.

Up here we could all see how much you were going through and it's crazy that nobody has ever sympathized with the difficulties of being with a widower with kids. It's great that everyone is being empathetic towards Roger and the children, but how about you? Don't you also have to deal with the husband and kids who are grieving? Even though life goes on for Roger and the kids, they're still grieving and you're going through it with them.

As I look back on the rough patches you had as a family, there are so many times that I wanted to step in. But with time, patience, and grace, you all have been working to make it through. I saw you were less involved with pushing to bring the family together, as it seemed the children came up with reasons to not be around you. You saw the problem and you started to look into separating from Roger so that he and the children could restore their relationship. I saw how that led to the explosive arguments you and Roger would have. But then I heard Roger tell you that no one was going to try to control the marriage and friendship he had with you. As his children's mother, I agreed with Roger. I have been watching you from afar, with a protective eye over my children and there was no abuse, no harm that you have inflicted on Tasha or Zack. I can't pinpoint the hatred other than you're not me. As I mentioned before, you and I are different and how we approach situations is different, but I yelled and disciplined the children just as you have. You have never physically touched my children in anger, so it's not like you have ever physically abused them.

I can attest that days, weeks, months, or years are not promised and you need to enjoy this life with Roger and have fun. Our children will find their way and we have given them the resources they need. Take it out of your hands and put it in God's hands. As you told Roger not long ago, our children are adults now, and they know right from wrong, and how to treat and not treat people.

Back in Zack's middle school days, you were hands-on. It was like you were in my shoes, keeping him on track in school. I thought you were awesome for doing that, but it made me so mad when my dad gave you a hard time helping my son in school. You asked him to come to the school and talk about Zack's grades and behavior with the principal. You didn't have to invite him, but you did so my dad could see you weren't just punishing Zack for nothing. You wanted Zack to see how not doing work , being disrespectful to teachers, and skipping school messes with his after-school activities. So, my dad came by your place after the school meeting, and he just wanted to make a fuss and argue with you. You didn't let him push you around, but I was so disappointed when he cursed you and almost started something we'd all regret. That's my dad and I love him, but you're strong, you stood up to him face to face. Luckily, Roger stepped in and told my dad to leave your house.

This is why I appreciate you being honest about therapy. Not everyone got the counseling or therapy they needed after I died, and emotions and feelings just went crazy. I guess you can see how much that situation hurt me. Everyone's different in how they express things, and my dad didn't like seeing you discipline Zack. One day, I hope he and my mom see that you're giving it you're all for the kids. Some people may not like you, but it's on them to figure out why they dislike someone who is looking out to help my kids, not hurt them. I mean, let's be honest about the situation. After my passing, so many people told Roger they would help him with the kids. Who reached out? You saw for yourself. So as Roger has said, and his mom said, who will be there will be there and that was you and a few others. I remember you Roger and Zack going to the grocery store and seeing my sister. She looked directly at Zack and headed down another aisle to avoid you and Roger. She refused to acknowledge Zack. I was there for it all and was so disappointed in my sister. Zack, literally had to run through the store to find her to say hi. So, again I would like to know why one would judge your efforts to help my kids. These are the things and actions that others and my kids included need to take a good look at and ask, why am I mad at this lady?

I understand why you were on board moving from Maryland to Florida. After you two got married, it was time to regroup and Roger's new job in Florida came right on time. You all needed a new beginning, away from your hurtful past. Moving did not solve all the problems, but it allowed you and Roger to reset in your own domain.

It was so nice to see you and Roger pull together the high school graduation party for Zack. You guys invited all our Maryland family, and many of them showed up. I loved how you also made sure my dad was comfortable. I also love how you are so pleasant to my aunt. She is my dad's baby sister, and she loves him and will go out of the way to make sure he is ok. I love seeing my dad and your dad talk. They like one another and that is good for the family.

Hey, I even showed up at the party. But you, Roger, and the kids screamed when you saw me. Remember the frog that somehow got in the house and stuck to the wall. That was me saying that everything was going to be alright. Funny, I understand you screaming, but I don't know why Roger and my kids were screaming. They knew it was me! Roger hurried to the kitchen to get a cup to put me in, and they did. That was one of our funny moments.

Now I see Tasha's getting used to the idea of her dad moving on. It took a while for her to go from calling you nothing but her dad's girlfriend, to reaching out for help with the kids. After she married, had four kids and now blended into a family of her own, her entire perspective has changed. I see her depending on you more and you welcoming her, especially as she navigates motherhood and raising step-kids. Thanks for helping her.

My youngest, who was unsure at first, is finding his way with your help. I know it's been tough dealing with a blended family, and not being included in on important matters. But I'm telling you, you have been a big help. And just so you know, I also look after your baby girl, Raya. She's family and I've got my arms around all our babies. She's a good girl who became a middle child and has been struggling with all the changes. When you and Roger married, I saw you present each person with a unity ring to seal the union between each one of you and bond you for life.

Now I see how the late-night conversations after my passing, the laughter shared over the phone, and the way you lean on each other's strengths have paid off. And even though some may not understand, I want you to know that I do. I see the purity of your intentions and the genuine love that you both share, and it brings me comfort. I encourage you to continue nurturing that bond, to embrace the simplicity of Roger's nature, and to fill your days with laughter. You are a lifeline for him, just as he is for you. I hope he continues to find comfort in the laughter that dances through your heart.

As it intertwines with yours, my life and legacy create a beautiful portrait of love and connection. Remember that night when you called upon me to help you with a situation that you suspected? Your intuition kicked in and some truths came to light that night. .

I know receiving this letter may be strange since I was the first woman who once held Roger's hand in marriage. But now that I am no longer on earth and Roger has moved on with you as his wife, please continue to love, heal, and thrive. You can't control what is not of you, so let go and let God take charge. You have done your part by showing hospitality to me and my family, and I be will forever appreciative of you.

With all my love and support,

Jerry

Southeast Nachos

This is a nacho dish that goes well with your Taco Tuesday main dish

Ingredients:

1 bag (about 10-12 ounces) tortilla chips

2 cups shredded cheddar cheese

2 cup shredded Monterey Jack cheese

1 cup cooked and diced grilled chicken breast

1/2 cup diced jalapenos (adjust to your spice preference)

1/2 cup diced red onion

1/2 cup diced tomato

1/2 cup chopped fresh cilantro

1/2 cup sour cream

1/4 cup sliced black olives

1/4 cup sliced green onions

Optional toppings: guacamole, salsa, hot sauce

Instructions:
1. Preheat your oven to 375°F (190°C).
2. Spread a layer of tortilla chips on a large baking sheet or oven-safe platter.
3. Sprinkle a generous layer of shredded cheddar and Monterey Jack cheese over the chips. Make sure to cover them evenly.

4. Evenly distribute the diced grilled chicken over the cheese-covered chips.

5. Sprinkle diced jalapenos, red onion, and tomato over the chicken and cheese.

6. Add another layer of shredded cheese to cover the toppings.

7. Place the baking sheet or platter in the preheated oven and bake for about 8-10 minutes, or until the cheese is fully melted and bubbly.

8. Garnish with chopped cilantro, sliced green onions, salsa, hot sauce sour cream and guacamole and Serve

DEAR FREDDI

ACKNOWLEDGMENTS

Thanks to God, his angels, and my support system for empowering me with the bravery to complete of this book. Not that long ago, I chose to improve my life and get support to face life's challenges.

I thank all the counselors, therapists, and coaches who have helped me along the way. All have provided useful tools and resources for getting through things.

I thank my family and friends for showing me grace, my parents for giving me life, and my FamBam for inspiring me in ways you can't imagine. I appreciate and love each of you.

To my husband, thank you! We're still rolling, and the wheels have not fallen off so let's keep going! You encourage me by allowing me to be me.

Freddi

DEAR FREDDI

FREDDI'S TOP 10 MENTAL HEALTH RESOURCES

1. Anxiety and Depression Association of America
   https://adaa.org
   The ADAA is a nonprofit organization that primarily directs its efforts towards anxiety disorders and depression.

2. American Psychiatric Association
   https://www.psychiatry.org
   The American Psychiatric Association is globally recognized as the foremost psychiatric association, with members spanning across more than 100 countries. The association strive to advance the world of psychiatry and provide the highest level of care to mental illness sufferers.

3. VA Mental Health Services
   https://www.va.gov/health-care/health-needs-conditions/mental-health
   Veterans can access VA mental health services for posttraumatic stress disorder (PTSD), psychological effects of military sexual trauma (MST), depression, grief, anxiety, and other needs.

4. National Alliance on Mental Illness (NAMI)
   https://www.nami.org
   NAMI is the United States' biggest grassroots mental health organization. It educates the population on mental illness with its education programs across the country. The alliance advocates mental health and runs the NAMI HelpLine.

5. American Foundation for Suicide Prevention
   800-273-TALK (1-800-273-8255) https://afsp.org
   The AFSP prevents suicide and provides support to those who have lost (or almost lost) someone to suicide.

6. Alcoholics Anonymous
   https://www.aa.org
   Alcoholics Anonymous is a fellowship of people who come together to solve their drinking problem. It doesn't cost anything to attend A.A. meetings.

7. The Anxiety Network
   https://anxietynetwork.com
   The Anxiety Network focuses on panic disorder, generalized anxiety disorder, and social anxiety disorder.

8. Born This Way Foundation
   https://bornthisway.foundation
   The Born This Way Foundation advocates mental wellness and empowerment. It targets young people, specifically, as the foundation knows that the creative and diverse young people of today are the future.

9. Depression and Bipolar Support Alliance
   https://www.dbsalliance.org
   DBSA is unique in that it was made for people with mood disorders and is run by people with mood disorders.

10. Families for Depression Awareness
    https://www.familyaware.org
    This organization aims to help families understand depression and bipolar disorder to better grasp the concept of mental illness and cope with it.

DEAR FREDDI

NOTE PAGES

DEAR FREDDI

DEAR FREDDI

DEAR FREDDI

DEAR FREDDI

DEAR FREDDI

DEAR FREDDI

DEAR FREDDI

DEAR FREDDI

DEAR FREDDI

DEAR FREDDI

OTHER BOOKS BY THE AUTHOR

1. Creating Your Lane: Unleashing Self-Confidence –
   August 10, 2022

2. Creating Your Lane: Launching Your Independent
   Travel Business– April 15, 2023